MW00574237

YOGA BUSINESS MASTERY

YOGA
BUSINESS
MASTERY

EARN A GREAT LIVING
DOING WHAT YOU LOVE

LUCAS ROCKWOOD

YB | PRACTICE IS
EVERYTHING

Hardcover ISBN: 978-1-5445-3184-7
Paperback ISBN: 978-1-5445-3183-0
Ebook ISBN: 978-1-5445-3182-3

Illustrations by Karina Diaz

To my loyal students,
who have faithfully turned up and
tuned in to my classes over the years;
I'm continually inspired by you.
Practice is everything.

Online Bonus Material

Get access to timely updates, price calculators,
new student forms, contract templates, and dozens
of other free resources exclusively for readers.

www.YogaBody.com/yogabusiness
password = business

Contents

Introduction xi

I.   Mindset Shift 1

II.   Skills and Certifications 15

III. Positioning for Success 37

IV. You + Your Community = Business 51

V.   Define Your Success 65

VI. Where to Teach (In-Person) 77

VII. How to Teach Online 93

VIII. Time Management 111

IX. Pricing and Packaging 125

X.   Your Online Profile 147

XI. Get the Gig 165

XII. How to Launch Your Business 185

Conclusion 199

Glossary 205

Introduction

I thought teaching yoga was a dropout job. I loved to practice, but it wasn't something I could envision as a career.

Back in 2003, I was living with my girlfriend, Clara, in Williamsburg, Brooklyn. I managed a vegan restaurant, while she worked from our living room as a hairdresser. We were both super into yoga. I practiced at Eddie Stern's shala on Broome Street in Manhattan every day before work. Clara was crazy for hot yoga. She was recently certified and taught a few classes per week at a studio in Midtown, in between her hairstyling clients.

One late summer evening, we were setting goals for the next year, and we both started buzzing about the idea of traveling around Southeast Asia for six months. At different stages of life, there are short windows of opportunity, and it was clear to us both that this chance probably wouldn't come again. "Why not?" we thought. "Let's do it."

Working in the restaurant industry, I was paid mostly in cash. Each week, I took a wad of bills, wrapped them with a rubber band, and threw them up on top of the kitchen cupboard. Clara did the same with her earnings, except she put her money in the freezer. It wasn't the safest way to save, but the weekly ritual was fun and helped build excitement.

One more week, one more wad of cash, one step closer to our goal.

For five months, that was my life—yoga, work, saving money. Pretty quickly, we had almost enough for the trip, and we started making concrete plans to escape New York for the adventure of a lifetime.

First, we needed to get rid of our stuff, so we held an ad hoc street sale and sold almost everything we owned. The proceeds allowed us to purchase two one-way tickets to Bangkok, which gave us a target date on the calendar. Our next step was to quit our jobs and tell our friends. Last, we stuffed all our remaining belongings into the travel backpacks propped up against the wall in our empty apartment. We could hardly believe it was happening.

When we landed in Bangkok, Clara immediately panicked. It was our first time in a developing country, and it was chaotic and intense. We'd left a nice $950 apartment, which was an absolute steal. We'd also left great jobs and a great group of friends. That first night, we stayed in a dodgy five-dollar-a-night hostel on Khao San Road, with no glass in the windows. The sink had no pipes and instead drained directly into a hole in the floor. In just twenty-four hours, our entire life had completely changed.

"Six months and I'm out of here," Clara said, swatting away a mosquito. "We're going back to New York."

Despite her initial misgivings, we pressed on with our plans. In the early days, I worked as an English teacher, which I hated. A one-hour session felt like an entire day's work. I hadn't planned on getting back into the restaurant industry, but it was something I knew well, and it was an easy fallback.

I was fortunate to get a job creating a menu for a local spa. I was also hired privately to prepare food for wealthy expats. Within months, I was even featured on the news talking about plant-based nutrition.

Sometimes in life, you get lucky and land in the right place at the right time. For me, Bangkok was all green lights. Everything was fun and easy. The only problem was that restaurant work wasn't going to allow me to travel and see the world the way I wanted to. I was making survival money but not enough to save.

What else could I do that would be more flexible? What about teaching yoga?

Clara was already teaching at one of the few studios in town, and I had previously taught a handful of donation classes back in New York. With my flimsy résumé and a big smile, I convinced the studio owner to give me a shot at teaching, even though I wasn't certified. I promised her that if things worked out, I would get properly trained within the next six months—and that's how I got my first real yoga job.

At that time, teaching yoga was still something I considered a temporary job. I needed a gig that would allow me to travel, and I thought, "Hey, maybe I can be a yoga teacher for a while."

During this period, Clara and I were living on just $1,200 a month, but we had a great life. I felt much wealthier teaching in Bangkok than I did earning good money in New York because I was doing something I loved and I had freedom. I could explore the beauty of Thailand on my days off, I wasn't feeling burned out, and my living expenses were so low that I could cover them by teaching just seven classes a week.

I wasn't a great teacher, but my classes quickly grew so full that students would overflow into the hallway. Before long, I was managing the studio where I taught, and, as promised, I soon took a formal yoga teacher training course. Suddenly, I was very much a real yoga teacher. It was a whirlwind experience.

Clara's initial unease transformed into a passion for travel and adventure. Our first six months quickly turned into a year, and although we loved Bangkok, we wanted to see more of Asia. One evening, we met a friend for dinner who had just arrived from Hong Kong, and she told us yoga was booming there. Once again, we thought, "Why not?"

Compared to other teachers, I was still pretty green, and it was a stretch to convince a studio in Hong Kong to sponsor me for a work visa and pay for my travel and accommodation expenses. But I pulled it off.

What I lacked in yoga experience, I made up for with professionalism. As you'll learn in Chapter XI, I was able to write a good email, I obtained a glowing reference from my previous employer, and I understood how to see the business from my prospective employer's perspective. Most yoga teachers flunk those basic prerequisites, so I stood out.

I landed the job, my girlfriend got a job too, and a month later we were again on a plane to a new adventure. Yoga, travel, rinse, repeat. And from here? The story continues with country after country, gig after gig, and tens of thousands of students, all the way up to the present day. Along the way, there have been yoga studios, products, TV shows, workshops, video courses, training courses, and more.

I discovered yoga has the potential to be much more than a dropout job. My travel gig turned into a career that I now consider my calling. I love learning, I love teaching, and this is my life's work.

Why Have You Picked Up This Book?

There are two groups of people who pick up this book. First, there are recently certified teachers excited to embark on a new career but scared to make the transition. If this is you, money is one of the biggest things holding you back. You might ask yourself, "Can I *really* earn a decent living with yoga?"

The second group consists of people who made the leap of faith long ago but are struggling financially and worried they might have made a bad decision. If this is you, you're likely wondering if there is a better way. "Is it possible to do the work I'm doing now but somehow double my income?"

As you know, most yoga teachers aren't exactly rolling in cash. If you take the average class rate in your area, multiplied by the average number of classes your peers are teaching each week, you'll find that their income doesn't meet your needs and desires long term. Could you live simply and manage with this income? Perhaps, but you didn't plan on working a survival job for decades, did you?

To complicate things, many new teachers are in a transitional phase of life. Maybe you're in the midst of a career crisis, or you've just ended (or started) an important relationship. Maybe your former lifestyle and social circle doesn't align with your future self. Or maybe you've realized the city where you're living now is not where you want to be in the future.

If you're like most new teachers looking to earn more money, your best idea is to teach more classes. I went down this path myself; at my peak, I was teaching twenty-one classes per week. I was making good money, sure, but nobody thought for a moment that was sustainable.

Teaching requires a high level of energy, at least twice as much as the average desk job. No one can consistently work a forty-hour week teaching. The solution is not to work more; it's to leverage your time so you have more growth potential.

I learned early on that most popular yoga business advice is horrible. My first trainer, for example, told me that if I wanted to make money, I should get a corporate job, not teach. Meanwhile, he was making six figures as a yoga teacher. And I thought, "Why not me?"

The majority of teachers live under the false belief that the yoga market is not a place to earn a decent income. Fortunately, research from the past three decades tells a very different story. The current yoga market is estimated at $37 billion and all indications suggest continued growth. If you're looking to create a stable teaching career, please know that there is both enough money and enough opportunity to go around.

But how do you get from where you are today to where you'd like to be next year? And in five years from now? There is no clear corporate ladder to climb. There's no board of directors you can turn to for sage advice, and there are no career placement programs.

If you want to build a career in yoga, you need to figure it out on your own. That's why I wrote this book—to aid you in that process. Undoubtedly, you have questions. How do I make this work and not end up in my fifties broke and single with no kids? How can I afford health insurance? Will I ever own a home? Should I open a studio, or is that a waste of money? What about teaching online?

We'll answer all those questions and more in this book, but first, let me ask you to imagine a stereotypical, successful yoga teacher. Who do you think of? Is it a twenty-something woman doing handstands on a beach with a million Instagram followers? Is it some super-fit teacher featured on a popular iPhone app? Or perhaps you're thinking of one of the big yoga websites run by Silicon Valley venture capitalists? If so, think again.

You may be shocked to learn that many of the celebrity teachers who come to mind are not making a lot of money. Worse still, their work life is boring. Most yoga teachers I meet want to teach, not create social media content all day, obsessing over the perfect pose to gather likes.

The good news is that some of the most successful yoga teachers in the world are low-profile people you've never heard of. For example, you'd probably never heard of me before picking up this book.

The yoga business is a lot like the music business. Very few musicians ever become pop stars; but for every star, there are hundreds of thousands of working professionals who make a great living from touring and recording sessions.

They do what they love, work where they want, and enjoy a wonderful lifestyle. The same is true in the yoga world.

In this book, you'll find a clear, practical guide to financial freedom and stability as a yoga teacher. You'll discover your unique abilities and pinpoint the services and gifts you have to offer your community. Together, we'll create a clear roadmap to get from where you are now to where you want to be as quickly as possible.

When I began teaching, all the job opportunities were controlled by yoga studio owners. Today, savvy yoga teachers call their own shots. You'll learn how to find teaching gigs, yes, but you'll also learn how to host your own classes, online or in person. You'll learn how to teach workshops, organize training events, create videos, and more. Right now is truly the best time in history to teach yoga, and you'll be excited to learn just how many opportunities are available.

Throughout the book, we'll alternate between strategy and tactics. The strategy pieces consist of high-level thinking that you can use to shape your yoga teaching business. The tactics are specific tools and actions you can put into practice right away with measurable, immediate results.

The book is designed to be read from cover to cover, but please feel free to skip sections and jump to the material most relevant to your situation right now. It's a hands-on reference to return to when a new challenge or unfamiliar scenario arises in your yoga teaching journey.

Why Should You Listen to Me?

There are thousands of established yoga teachers in the world, so you're probably wondering, "Does this guy know what he's talking about?" As I mentioned above, I started teaching in 2003 before I was certified. After I received a certification, I embarked on what I can only describe as a teaching binge. Most of my early teaching career took place in Southeast Asia, in the countries of Thailand, Hong Kong, and Singapore. At one point, I was teaching three or four classes per day.

In 2006, I opened my first studio, taught my first workshop, and launched my first training series. Since then, I've owned a total of four studios outright and franchised or co-owned another three studios in five different countries. I've certified more than twenty-one thousand teachers and delivered a TEDx Talk on yoga breathing, which has been viewed more than two million times.

During my teaching tenure, I've managed to live the kind of grounded life that escapes many of my colleagues. I've gainfully employed more than 150 teachers and staff. I have three kids. I have health insurance. I now call Barcelona, Spain my home. My client list ranges from everyday people trying to improve their health to high-profile clients such as Facebook and Noom, for which I run corporate wellness events.

I'm sharing this with you because I want you to know that whatever your aspirations, they're likely more attainable than you realize. I'm the quintessential yoga bum. If I can carve out a successful yoga teaching career using the lessons in this book, there's a very good chance you can do the same.

Why Write a Book?

You may be wondering why I've chosen to share everything I know about the yoga business in the pages of a book. If my teaching business is going so well, why not focus on that? First, I *am* actively teaching yoga at a blistering pace. I'm more passionate about teaching than ever before. The reason I'm putting so much time into business resources is because a huge thrust of my career right now is yoga teacher training courses.

If my graduates succeed in their training but not in business, then I consider the whole venture to be a flop. I want to train tomorrow's teachers who will also need to be business leaders. From a job satisfaction point of view, what lights me up more than anything else is when teachers graduate from my courses and go on to do bigger and better things than I could ever do myself—something that happens constantly.

It's true that from a financial perspective, putting my best advice into an inexpensive book might not be the smartest choice, but I know that for every one student who joins me live online or in person, there are at least ten others who cannot afford the investment in my courses. Hopefully, this book format will make my teachings accessible to just about anyone.

The last reason I decided to write a book is because the yoga industry is not taken seriously. It sees more than its fair share of high-profile bankruptcies, like Yoga Works, and shameful sex scandals, which seem to be a constant fixture of news cycles. Industry-wide, the lack of professionalism is frankly embarrassing, particularly for someone like me who is committed to yoga as a career. Lack of business training and professionalism are not the only problems, of course, but my hope is that this book, in some small way, helps shift the industry for the better.

My Goals for You

I hope you'll use this book to create a life of meaning, significance, and financial stability on your own terms. As an independent teaching professional, I want you to control where you live and who you work with. I'd like to help you develop a career that truly matches who you are.

I should make it clear that you won't find anything in these pages about SEO, pay-per-click marketing, or influencer deals. I don't believe in personal branding and will actively discourage you from owning your own studio.

The objective of this book is both more humble and more lucrative. I want you to become a hero in the eyes of your clients. I want them to appreciate the difference you've made in their lives. I want you to do what you're already doing, teaching excellent classes, but I want you to earn a great living doing it.

Let's get started.

CHAPTER I

Mindset Shift

In 2004, I had a very relaxed schedule. I taught a ten o'clock Power Yoga class on weekday mornings and an Ashtanga Primary series class on Thursday and Saturday evenings. I made around $30 an hour, which is not bad at all in Bangkok, but after just a month of hanging out with my fellow teachers, I adopted the negative money mindset that pervades the yoga community.

First, I started resenting studio owners. They must be making a fortune, I thought, and there I was, making only $210 per week! When I didn't get my ideal teaching schedule, I complained that there were too many teachers and not enough opportunities to go around. Last, and this is so embarrassing, I started preaching that yoga should be free and that no one wants to pay for it anyway. Wow, that escalated fast.

Keep in mind, I was working less than ten hours a week and was as green as they come. The industry had offered me nothing but great opportunities every step of the way, and my hourly rate was totally decent by anyone's standards. So why all the negativity?

I now understand that when you're underemployed and underearning, it can make you angry and irrational. Your head gets filled with negative trash, and that's exactly what happened to me. Of course, I wasn't making as much as I did when I worked an office job. I was hardly working at all. What did I expect?

If you've ever felt this way, I have good news. This poverty thinking in yoga is categorically false. The yoga market has been growing by 10 percent (or more) each year for over three decades. It's not a fad or a bubble; it's a global wellness movement that started catching steam in the '90s and is now a $37 billion industry that shows no signs of slowing.

To grow your teaching business, it's crucial that your mindset is aligned with the reality of this exciting industry. In this chapter, we'll work to clear negativity and add positive inputs to get you and keep you on track for a successful future.

Empty Your Head Trash

When head trash dominates your inner dialogue, it has so many things to say about why the yoga market is broken. Underneath it all, however, the fundamental message is the same: no you can't, no you won't, you're not good enough, there's not enough money, there aren't enough opportunities, give it up, get a real job.

Is the market really saturated with teachers? No, quite the opposite. Studios are desperate to attract and hire professional teachers. If you don't believe me, next time you're at your local yoga studio, just ask the owner what their biggest challenge is. They'll tell you it's finding and retaining high-quality staff. Also, keep in mind that since 2012, the market has shifted, with more yoga jobs now offered outside of yoga studios than inside. When you start looking with the right mindset, there are opportunities everywhere.

But what about the hundred thousand-plus newly certified yoga teachers each year? Those new teachers must be competing for your jobs, right? No, not at all. Most teacher training programs don't train teachers. They offer immersive yoga courses where people are given a piece of paper at the end. No one at those courses, not the students or the trainers, have any misconceptions. The course is a fun, personal growth experience, not a vocational training.

Ninety-seven percent of certified yoga teachers don't go on to teach. This means that for the millions of new students entering the yoga world each year, there are only a few thousand new teachers able to meet this growing demand. Huge demand coupled with a limited supply of instructors is one of the reasons I've been so successful, and it's also a big part of the reason I've written this book.

Opportunities are everywhere, professional teachers are scarce, and the market needs you. Don't let uninformed opinions cloud your vision of what is possible for you as a yoga teacher. In case you're still skeptical, allow me to dismantle some of the most common objections I hear.

"YOGA TEACHERS ARE PAID SO BADLY."

At the time of writing, the average yoga teacher in the United States makes forty dollars per hour. If you're in a smaller city, it might be a bit lower. Meanwhile, if you live in New York City, Sydney, or London, it could be much, much more. Based on average earnings nationally and internationally, any way you slice it, this is more than double the median hourly income.

The challenge is *not* that yoga teacher pay is low. The challenge is that many teachers are underemployed and underearning, just like I was. To complicate things, live classes drain your energy, making an eight-hour teaching day impossible. We'll solve this energy problem later in the book, but when it comes to mindset, you need to stop saying yoga teachers are poorly paid. It's simply not true.

"BUT I DON'T HAVE ENOUGH FOLLOWERS!"

Struggling teachers often lament that they lack the social media following required to earn what they deserve. Today, I have a relatively large social following, but I'll be the first to tell you that unless you want to enter into brand partnership with an eco-deodorant or write sponsored posts for a coconut water company, it doesn't matter. Other than potential marketing partners, who cares? Not your students, that's for sure.

I use social media daily, and so should you, but I use it to connect with my students, answer questions, and teach. Two years ago, I deleted all five thousand of my friends on Facebook. More recently, I closed an Instagram account with over one hundred thousand followers—*poof*, it was gone. Why? Both were a waste of time and were distracting me from my core business: teaching. At the end of the day, I work for myself, not Big Tech, and you should too. If you don't have a big social media presence now, don't worry at all.

"NO ONE PAYS FOR YOGA ANYMORE; EVERYTHING IS FREE ONLINE."

Free yoga videos have exploded online, and some are excellent. The limiting belief here is that these free videos are enough and students will stop paying. This is not true. I've been practicing since 2002, and the word *enough* has never entered my vocabulary when it comes to yoga. Has it entered yours?

As a passionate yoga student, it's not about choosing this or that, free or paid; it's about all of it. I want the thick, extra-wide yoga mat for home practice, but I also have an ultralight foldable mat for travel. I want to learn the Ashtanga Primary series one day, and then I want a deep stretching class the next week.

For yoga people like me, the answer is always "more." As a teacher and trainer, I'm happy to report that all that free content simply expands the yoga market and drives more and more people to paid programs.

"WITH SO MANY ONLINE CLASSES AVAILABLE, STUDENTS WILL CHOOSE THE MOST FAMOUS TEACHERS."

In 2020, when yoga made a seismic shift online, I worried that famous teachers would siphon off all my students. In many ways, those media figures were younger, fitter, and more capable than me.

You know what happened? Just the opposite. The entire market splintered into highly specialized classes. Meritocracy, rather than fame, determined success. Today, I teach bigger classes and run a more successful business than teachers who are a hundred times more famous than me.

If you don't believe me, think about the music industry, where the same shift occurred a decade earlier. When streaming services like Spotify and Apple Music appeared, did all the listens go to the top fifty artists? No, the entire market suddenly spread out, and smaller artists found new audiences and reached hundreds of thousands of plays per month—a revolution!

Remember this: some of the most impactful yoga teachers, making great money, are people you've never heard of. Online yoga allows great teachers of all types to shine.

"BUT I'M NOT _____ ENOUGH!"

I've heard every imaginable excuse in this category. "I'm not young enough," "I'm not thin enough," "I'm not flexible enough," "I'm not business-oriented enough," "I'm not extroverted enough."

We all have things we would like to improve, and we also have problems and weaknesses. So what? Are there big holes in your teaching ability or your business acumen? Probably, but since you're reading this book, that tells me you already have enough knowledge to get started, and you can learn the rest as you go. Forget about perfect; it'll never happen. Strive to improve day by day, and let's get to work.

"BUT I DON'T EVEN CARE ABOUT MONEY."

I used to denounce money as a necessary evil, as something only greedy people prioritized. I wanted to focus on living, not wealth; freedom, not bills. I was young and naive, and I now understand that when someone says they don't care about money, what they're actually saying is that someone else cares about money for them: a parent, a partner, a spouse, or a social security system.

During a self-righteous conversation with my brother, I shared my go-with-the-flow views on money. He was paying $1,700 a month for his family's health insurance, and I was flabbergasted. Why not use that money to travel? You could live a great life in Bangkok for that amount of money, I told him. At that point, I'd gone six years without health insurance, and I was just fine.

His response shifted my perspective forever.

"You not having health insurance basically means you've outsourced the problem to the rest of us. If you get sick, you'll bankrupt me and the entire family."

If you still think you don't care about money, I'd encourage you to think about the people in your life who are or will be responsible if something happens. Money matters. As mature adults, we all need to contribute, earn, and openly discuss finances.

"THE YOGA BUSINESS IS CONTROLLED BY RICH PEOPLE."

Reality check. Take a look at the phone in your pocket and then do a Google search for how much you paid for it. The cost of your phone is more than the average annual income in twenty countries and over half the annual income in a dozen more. If you're worried that wealthy people control yoga, then you should feel fortunate because you are one of those wealthy people.

Your financial privilege is unprecedented in history. You won the life lottery. I don't care how cash poor you are today or how much debt you have. It doesn't matter if your home is in foreclosure or even if you're in the middle of a bankruptcy. If your great-grandparents saw how comfy and luxurious your life is today, they would fall over backwards! Just imagine what they would say when you told them you get paid forty to seventy dollars an hour for teaching a group yoga class!

We've completely lost perspective.

There are no big players in the yoga market, meaning people like you and me can build amazing businesses. Some analysts believe that in the next couple of years, the market will grow to a whopping $66 billion. There is more than enough money to go around. There is space for you, and the opportunities are expanding.

"ONLY STUDIO OWNERS MAKE MONEY IN THE INDUSTRY."

Studio ownership used to be a great way to earn a living, but that era ended years ago. As the yoga market expanded, the prices of yoga studio memberships dropped so low that it costs less today to purchase one than it did twenty years ago. I know that seems hard to believe, but from New York to Bangkok, yoga memberships are cheaper now than they were at the turn of the century, despite operating costs nearly doubling in that same period.

Most studio owners barely cover their bills, and many lose money each month. It's common in the industry for studio owners to pay bills from their savings or from other non-yoga jobs.

I knew a business analyst who conducted extensive market research himself, independently, and he determined that the average profitable studio earned its owner about $40,000 per year before taxes. Most of those owners were teaching, managing, marketing, and promoting their studios as well. Many even cleaned the floors.

They were working sixty-plus hours per week, taking on enormous debt and risk, and at the end of the day, they were making about the same hourly wage as an entry-level server at the restaurant down the street.

Yoga Works, the first yoga studio publicly traded on the stock market, went bankrupt in 2020. They had one-hundred-plus locations and were in business for over thirty years, yet they didn't survive. To me, this signaled the end of an era. Brick-and-mortar studios are a dying breed.

This news pains me more than anyone. I love yoga studios, and I spent the majority of my money and a huge chunk of my career building them. Sadly, that ship has sailed. The math doesn't work anymore and it's time to let it go. In almost all cases, the star teacher at the local yoga studio can make more than the studio owner can. I want that star teacher to be you.

"I LOVE YOGA, BUT IT'S NOT A GOOD CAREER CHOICE."

CNN Money conducted a survey of the most desirable jobs in the United States, and yoga teacher came in at number ten. The median salary for a senior yoga teacher in the study was $62,000 per year, while the highest-paid teachers earned $119,000. Yoga teaching received an A rating for job satisfaction, benefit to society, and low levels of stress. Still think yoga is not a good career choice? If you know what you're doing and have a plan, it's an excellent choice.

Find Five Inspirations

An important part of changing your mindset is changing the people in your sphere of influence. As the saying goes, you become the average of the five people you spend the most time with, and although that might be true, most of us are unable to swap out our negative friends and relatives at the drop of a hat—nor would we want to.

Nonetheless, in order to clear our head trash and reframe our mindset for success, we do need better influences in our lives. That goes for yoga as much as any other career path. To build a stable of positive influences, your assignment is to add five inspirational people to your life as quickly as possible.

When I first started teaching yoga, my colleagues were all anti-business. I didn't have access to anyone else, so I turned to the internet. On LinkedIn, I quickly found an entrepreneur who was seven years older than me. She ran an impressive yoga teaching business traveling around Southeast Asia. I followed her and sent her a message. She was my first inspiration.

Next, I discovered one of her connections who was equally successful, although her teaching focused more on corporate wellness. To start with, I studied her marketing, teaching calendar, and promotions. I then sent her a quick email to open a dialogue. It looked like this:

> *Hello Kelly—I was really inspired to read that you left corpo-*
> *rate banking to launch your yoga wellness program. I worked*

*in publishing and then the restaurant industry before I made
the leap to yoga. To be honest, I am still figuring things out
business-wise, but I'm excited for what comes next.*

I just wanted you to know I'm inspired by your story. Congrats!

All the best,

Lucas

Kelly was flattered and responded the next day. As it turns out, she had some website questions I was able to help with, and we went on to exchange a series of emails over the next few months. One of the biggest things she taught me was the importance of registration deadlines for workshops and events (we'll cover this in Chapter IX).

My third inspiration was a martial arts instructor who was teaching via his website. I admired his ability to use email as a teaching tool, and I was excited to try it with yoga. I followed all his blogs and bought his books. Although we never met in person, we exchanged emails, and his ideas inspired many of my initial emails to my community.

Last, I did a deep dive with Dale Carnegie and Jim Rohn, two old-school personal development teachers who were both early inspirations for me. I read their books, listened to old conference recordings, and soaked up everything I could get my hands on. In this way, I connected with five people (and eventually many more) who helped me build a success mindset. Out with the negativity, in with a positive future focus.

Now it's your turn. Mark some time on your calendar to find five inspiring people to follow and to potentially meet in person.

These five people could be colleagues in the industry or even in another field. They should be at least three to five years further along in their career than you, and they should inspire you to be your best in specific areas where you need help.

If you can meet them in person, that's amazing, but let's assume for now that you cannot. Find inspiration online, follow their accounts, and send them an email or a message like I did to open the door for conversations.

A word of warning: when you decide to actively create positive change in your life, friends and family may feel threatened or judged. I remember when I enrolled in a $700 personal growth workshop and told two of my fellow yoga teachers. They both laughed and told me I'd been scammed. I now understand that they were just jealous of how fast my business was growing. Fourteen years later, those same two teachers are in the same place, doing the same job, making the same income.

So let other people laugh, or simply don't tell them what you're up to. As long as you're taking the necessary steps, it doesn't matter. Just remember, a success mindset is the crucial base for everything you want to build.

Fix Your Mindset, Then Launch

I had a student named Bettina. When she discovered yoga, she soon stopped drinking, lost weight, and turned her life around. She quit her bartending job to enroll in our teacher training course, and shortly after graduation, she landed a very steady teaching gig at a local studio.

She loved the work, but she wasn't making nearly as much as she had in the bar.

When she went through my business training, she lit up with ideas and was excited to finally increase her earnings by teaching a quarterly workshop series on yoga for back pain—but then she became infected with a negative mindset.

Bettina had pitched the workshop idea to her boss, who promptly shut it down. He didn't think enough people would enroll in such a narrowly focused workshop. Bettina was completely deflated and asked one of her fellow teachers for a second opinion. Again, she received a negative response.

I explained to Bettina that her colleagues were wrong. Back pain is such a big problem that the back pain market is actually larger than the entire yoga market. Bettina understood intellectually, but emotionally she was still paralyzed. The only way out was to add in some real-world inspiration. I gave Bettina the same assignment I'm giving you in this chapter: go out and find five people who are doing things you want to do.

Bettina spent thirty minutes on social media and found no fewer than three teachers in different cities teaching almost exactly what she wanted to offer. She couldn't believe it.

From the teachers' photos and online reviews, it was clear that these workshops were successful and well attended. Bettina quickly gleaned some small but important details about schedule and pricing that she incorporated into her soon-to-be workshop. Excited, she emailed all three teachers, and one of them was kind enough to join a short phone conversation to answer questions. After that call, Bettina was on fire again.

Armed with a positive mindset, Bettina approached three local gyms the same day, and two of them said yes. Her first weekend workshop launched a month later with eight students, and the second launched six weeks later, attracting seventeen people. Her initial goal was to increase her monthly income by 20 percent, and she managed to bring in an extra 23 percent—even better! The workshop idea was always a great one, but without fixing her mindset, Bettina would never have gotten started.

CHAPTER II

Skills and Certifications

In 2002, I managed a large vegan restaurant in New York City. I loved all things yoga, so I coordinated donation-based classes in a back room.

One Tuesday, the scheduled teacher called in sick, minutes before her class was due to begin. As I've come to learn, this happens often. I had just two options: teach the class myself or cancel it. Three students were already waiting in the back, so I decided to teach, even though I had zero experience and was wearing jeans.

The class was a clumsy, stutter-stop-start attempt for me to get them through a handful of postures. Denim and triangle pose are not a good mix. To make things worse, the restaurant waitstaff interrupted me once to get approval for a reservation and a second time to get a signature for a vegetable delivery.

To my credit, I survived. The students were gracious and even left a few dollars in the donation box by the exit. I wasn't proud of my teaching skills that day, but I'd broken through the psychological barrier that stands between many would-be teachers and their first class. I'd proven that I was a capable teacher, even with no certification and no fancy yoga clothes.

I'd just started my career in the restaurant business, so I'd never considered teaching yoga; but there it was, another possibility for the next chapter of my life that I couldn't ignore.

From that small seed, my yoga teaching career began to flourish. With one session under my belt, our regular teacher called on me as her backup more and more often and I quickly logged half a dozen sessions as her substitute. To promote those classes, I posted black-and-white flyers on the bulletin boards at local health food stores in the East Village. I made sure to have a set of yoga clothes at work so that whenever I needed to, I could step in and lead a class. Attendance was small, of course, but the same people came back again and again.

We all start from zero, and this was my start. From that first Tuesday class until today, my skills and qualifications have grown exponentially through deliberate practice. Learning to teach is not a fixed destination; it's a lifelong journey.

With that in mind, let's examine the certifications and skills most relevant for you today, and let's identify the areas in which you need to grow to take your teaching business to the next level.

Yoga Teacher Certifications

To grow your teaching business, you'll inevitably want to continue your studies. Most career teachers I know take at least thirty hours of additional training per year to deepen their expertise. I'll be the first to tell you that skills, not certificates, should be your top priority—but let's first review the leading registries and organizations so you can better understand the training landscape, and then we'll explore the most-relevant skills needed to stand out in the marketplace.

YOGA ALLIANCE

Yoga Alliance is the leading trade registry for the market. Membership is for schools and teachers, and it's application only. Yoga Alliance offers access to some interesting professional resources.

YogaAlliance.org is the website of the original Yoga Alliance nonprofit, based in the United States. YogaAllianceProfessionals.org is a similar organization with a strong presence in the United Kingdom. Additionally, there are a handful of Yoga Alliance organizations in Canada, Australia, New Zealand, and India, but the vast majority of yoga schools worldwide default to being part of the US or UK groups.

Here's how it works for schools. Yoga training schools apply for their course(s) to be reviewed and approved. If accepted, they pay an annual fee and are then allowed to issue certificates to their graduates.

The application process for training schools has become more and more rigorous over the years, and although it's often criticized, I've always supported the Yoga Alliance organizations and believe they are doing their best to improve yoga teaching standards.

Here's how it works for teachers. When you graduate from a registered school, you can also join the Yoga Alliance registry. Since registration involves some paperwork and an annual fee, many yoga teachers don't get around to registering until the need arises.

When might the need arise? Some studios will require you to be registered to teach there. Some insurance providers will require you to be registered to provide you with cover. If you travel and teach, you might need to show proof of a formal teacher certification to obtain a work visa.

Approximately 95 percent of yoga teachers in studios and gyms were trained at the 200-hour level. This typically takes four weeks full time or eight to twelve weeks part time. Many ambitious yoga teachers assume that if they obtain a 250-hour, 300-hour, or 500-hour certification, it will give them an advantage, but I've never seen this occur.

If you happen to have a higher level of certification, that's great. If you're uncertified, that's also fine, and if you have a collection of both certified and uncertified training experiences—the most common situation—that's great too.

To understand certification in yoga, it's helpful to draw another parallel to the music industry. Bruno Mars is an amazing musician, and he never went to music school. Miles Davis is equally remarkable, and he went to the esteemed Institute of Musical Arts (now Juilliard). Did that hurt Bruno? Did it help Miles?

Some of the most successful yoga teachers in history ignored or even denounced Yoga Alliance. My professional opinion is that you should only join a training course you believe will make you a better teaching professional. At the end of the day, your goal should be to master your craft, not to collect certificates on the wall.

AMERICAN COUNCIL ON EDUCATION (ACE)

The American Council on Education is an accreditation organization that formally reviews undergraduate-level course materials, exam procedures, ethics policies, and teaching faculty. The process takes many months and includes a formal review by a board of university-level professors. Only a handful of yoga courses in the world have undergone this review.

AMERICAN COUNCIL ON EXERCISE (ACE)

The American Council on Exercise is a health and fitness accreditation organization that reviews yoga and fitness courses and approves them for professional-level training.

INTERNATIONAL COACH FEDERATION (ICF)

The ICF is a global organization for coaches and coaching. The ICF is dedicated to advancing the coaching profession by setting high standards, providing independent certification, and building a worldwide network of trained coaching professionals.

NATIONAL ACADEMY OF SPORTS MEDICINE (NASM) AND ATHLETICS AND FITNESS ASSOCIATION OF AMERICA (AFAA)

The NASM and AFAA are accreditation organizations designed to provide continuing education opportunities, primarily for personal trainers but also for a growing number of yoga schools.

Beware of "Certificate-itis"

Certificate-itis is an industry term for would-be teachers who are addicted to certification courses. Instead of pursuing paid work, they continuously sign up for course after course. Instead of putting themselves out there professionally, they get stuck forever in student mode.

I've had certificate-itis many times. Left to my own devices, I'd do nothing but take course after course, class after class. At one point, I had memberships at three different studios simultaneously! In the yoga world, it's not uncommon to meet people who are certified as yoga teachers, personal trainers, Thai massage therapists, reiki masters, and mindfulness coaches. They are a veritable one-stop shop for mind-body wellness. They've spent thousands of hours (and dollars) studying, and yet they've never taught a single class.

Worse still, the more qualified they become without any real-world experience, the more intimidating it is for them to finally start.

If you can teach a class, even if it's a little wobbly, even if you're wearing jeans, and even if no third party has given you approval, then you need to start teaching right now. Keep learning, but start teaching.

I'm the founder of one of the largest yoga training schools in the world, so you might find it strange that I'm telling you to stop chasing certificates, but there's a big difference between collecting diplomas and learning to teach. Every course I lead, I aim to share real-world skills, not to give my students letters after their names. All great teachers are lifelong learners, but the best instructors focus on their craft first and foremost. Let's take a closer look at the skills most relevant to your career.

Are You Ready?

Here's a quick self-assessment exercise to help you gauge where you are in your career:

1. Have you taken approximately twenty classes as a student?

2. Have you taught at least twenty-five public classes?

3. Do you have the skills and abilities to lead a safe and effective class?

4. Can you teach an effective sixty-, seventy-five-, or ninety-minute class?

5. Have you participated in a general teacher training program?

If you can answer yes to at least three of these questions, you have enough skills to start your yoga business right now.

THE SKILL OF LEADERSHIP

Leadership in yoga is built on three pillars: practice, preparation, and experience. With strong leadership skills, you'll command authority, build and maintain trust, and serve as the benevolent leader of your students. Strong leaders can manage a class of any size, online or offline, indoors or outdoors.

A strong leader clearly shows that they've practiced what they are teaching hundreds of times. They are prepared and organized for their sessions, and their experience shows. For obvious reasons, no one can show up with perfect leadership every class, but we should strive for it.

A poor leader often leaves their students confused, disorganized, and doubting their competency. You might see students doing their own thing, checking their phones, talking, or even walking out of the room. Sometimes, students are conscious of their teacher's lack of leadership; more often, they sense it unconsciously and simply tune out, waiting for the class to end.

I knew a teacher named David who had exceptional leadership skills. I saw him manage a workshop where the group was so large that it was difficult for him to be seen or heard. But when David whistled and gestured for all ninety of us to come join him in the corner of the studio, we all stopped what we were doing and stepped in close.

When David put us into groups of three and talked us through a safe partner-assisted handstand, we all followed his lead, and most of us went upside down for the very first time ever.

Leadership is not a trick or a certificate; it's something you consciously develop by leaning into the three pillars of practice, preparation, and experience.

Q: How are your leadership skills? How is your practice, preparation, and experience when it comes to your classes? When you walk into a room and everyone is talking, are you able to gather attention and take control? When you give instructions, are people leaning in and listening, or do you find it difficult to hold focus?

COMMUNICATION SKILLS

Effective communication in yoga involves both your voice and your body. To teach a complex sun salutation or a headstand, you need to carefully select words and pair them with gestures or even an occasional demonstration. This is an unusual skillset.

There are some teachers who speak very well but are physically frozen. Others demonstrate beautifully but cannot speak like a professional. The best teachers dance between showing and telling, combining their gestures or demonstrations with verbal instructions.

I used to practice with a world-renowned teacher, a household name in the yoga world. He would teach with his hands clasped behind his back or interlaced in front of his waist. He did this so often that you'll see him standing in this very position in nearly every photo.

And what about his verbal skills? He was a decent speaker but not great. Mostly, he just called out pose names and counted. Despite his fame, which he inherited rather than earned, he was not a very effective teacher.

Juxtapose that with another early teacher of mine who was deaf. Since she knew her voice was hard to understand, she chose every word carefully. Her first language was sign language, so she was no stranger to gestures. Physically, she was one of the best teachers I've ever practiced with—and that doesn't mean she was stuck at the front of the room demonstrating. Quite the opposite. Every word was accompanied by a movement, every verbal cue included a physical teaching tip as well. She would point, lift her hands as we inhaled, puff her chest to illustrate up dog, and physically pantomime movements while walking around the room.

She might not be as famous as that other teacher I mentioned, but she was a superior communicator and had no problem filling a room. Her teaching business was doing just great.

To improve your verbal and nonverbal communication skills, I encourage you to try teaching yoga to kids younger than five. Kids' vocabularies are limited, which means you'll need to use simple, direct, carefully chosen words, and you'll need to calibrate your body and gestures like an elementary school teacher (schoolteachers are great verbal and nonverbal communicators, by the way).

Q: How are your communication skills? Do you find yourself relying solely on your words or stuck on your mat demonstrating everything? Do you find yourself thinking, "Why don't they get it?" and becoming frustrated by how students misunderstand? Remember that communication skills in yoga always include both showing and telling.

INTERPERSONAL SKILLS

A yoga teacher with strong interpersonal skills can give and receive feedback with grace. They are patient even when students ask repetitive and redundant questions. They are good listeners and try to be responsive rather than reactive.

I'm an introvert and socially anxious, so interpersonal skills have always been challenging for me, and any strides I've made in this area have been hard-earned.

I used to say, "I'm bad at names." Now I learn everyone's name. I used to spin out with anxiety whenever I received critical feedback. Now I listen quietly and take the feedback home with me so I can think it through carefully when I have space. I used to give students harsh feedback in classes, focused more on what was right than what was tactful. Now I've learned to sandwich criticisms with compliments so students don't feel like they're being attacked for having bad alignment.

The best resource I've ever found for improving your interpersonal skills is the book *How to Win Friends and Influence People* by Dale Carnegie. It's one of the few books I've read multiple times, and it's completely changed the way I work with my students.

Q: How are your interpersonal skills? Do you learn names? Are you able to take critical feedback? Are you a good listener? Can your classes be serious and fun (even funny) during the same session? Are you easy to be around, or do you and the people in your vicinity walk on eggshells?

MOTIVATION SKILLS

A colleague once told me, "Your clients are renting your motivation for the hour they are with you." She must be right because otherwise, why would students show up to class in the first place? Why not just access the thousands of free videos on YouTube?

Our intrinsic motivation lets us down constantly. To overcome this, we need a push from outside, which is why we pay teachers to lend us their motivation for the duration of the class. And what if your teacher doesn't have much motivation to begin with? What if their work ethic and commitment to their practice is less than yours? If this happens, that teacher's career is in trouble.

Everyone finds motivation from different sources, but the most reliable source is your personal practice and direct experiences. If you're committed to your own journey as a student of yoga, that will transmit directly into your teaching. When your yoga practice is working for you, you'll naturally want to share it with others. With that in mind, when you lack motivation, the simple solution is to roll out your mat and practice.

Q: Are you actively walking your talk? Do you personally do the practices you teach, or are you just phoning it in? We all have good days and bad days, but on average, are you someone your students can look up to because of your admirable work ethic and motivation?

TEAMWORK SKILLS

Yoga teachers mostly work alone. Once the door closes and class starts, it's just you and your students. No team, no backup, no plan B. Growing your business, however, is a completely different world. You'll need to work well with studio owners, gym managers, staff, and event organizers. If you're a team player in the yoga business, it means you're easy to work with, solution-oriented, reliable, and communicative.

I knew a teacher named Raquel who had a huge following on social media and was very much a one-woman show. Her social media posts were great. Her content was honest, inspiring, and educational, but she struggled to make money as an influencer. To solve this problem, she decided to go on a worldwide studio teaching tour—on the face of it, a great idea! The only snag was that Raquel was hell to work with. She demanded prepayment a month in advance, answered emails days after they were sent, and did things her own way or not at all.

At a friend's studio where she was scheduled for a workshop, she showed up three minutes before her sold-out class, wearing a full face of makeup, and refused to do any postures because she was worried her mascara would run. She ignored the studio owner's request not to take photos of students without permission and stopped every ten minutes to film a selfie video. The entire class was horribly awkward.

She was a good teacher with a big audience, but her teamwork was nonexistent. This was her first and last teaching tour. Truthfully, the students seemed unfazed. They loved her regardless. But not a single studio has invited her back to teach again, even many years later.

So how do you become better at teamwork? Always remember that even when you're working alone, you're working for your students and with studio owners, venues, and partners. Although you might feel like a one-person show, the best teachers are collaborative and focus on service first. I'm not suggesting you let people take advantage of you, but I am reminding you that you need to always care for the needs of your clients and your employers, or you won't have any.

Q: If I were to ask the studio owners and teachers with whom you work, how would they describe your teamwork? Are you reliable? Trustworthy? Responsive? Are you willing to help out in a pinch? If a problem arises, can they count on you? Are you a one-person show, or are you willing to collaborate and compromise when needed?

PROBLEM-SOLVING SKILLS

If you teach yoga long enough, pretty much everything you can imagine will happen in your classes: marital spats, slips and falls, power outages, overflowing toilets, gag-inducing body odor, burglaries, and more. Many of the problems yoga teachers face are not yoga-related. They are random life challenges that show up at 7:13 p.m. on any given Tuesday, during your Power Flow class.

I had a colleague, Matt, who saw three men lingering outside the studio where he was about to teach. They were in hoodies, smoking cigarettes, and he thought they looked suspicious and definitely not like yoga students. So he gathered his things, locked the studio, and went home, canceling the class. Was Matt's intuition about those three men correct? Who knows, but we can all agree his problem-solving skills were horrible. The studio owner was irate, the students were all standing outside in the cold for thirty minutes, and Matt was nowhere to be found.

I worked with another teacher named Jen who was an absolute pro. On one occasion, a student fainted in her class due to dehydration. Without missing a beat, she cued the other students in class to take child's pose. She then waved the receptionist in to help, and the two of them quietly removed the woozy student from the practice room.

Jen then asked one of her students in the front row to lead the next few poses. Out in the lobby, once it was clear the student was just fine, Jen went back and explained the situation. Everyone applauded, and she finished the class on time. That's problem solving in yoga, and it's a skill you need if you're planning to teach long term.

To accelerate your learning, I'd encourage you to take on more responsibilities inside and outside of the yoga room. I have a friend who volunteers at a women's shelter, and her problem-solving skills are challenged every week. I have a graduate who works with kids with ADHD in an after-school yoga program, and every day is a problem-solving day. Get outside your comfort zone and try something new. You'll become a better problem solver and a better teacher because of it.

Q: Do you struggle to solve problems? Do you find yourself freezing or bailing out when things go wrong? What kinds of problems have you encountered in your teaching so far? Are you happy with the way you handled it? Could you improve in the future?

PUBLIC SPEAKING SKILLS

The greatest teaching tool in yoga is your voice, so public speaking skills are crucial. My natural speaking voice is nasally. I mumble and laugh nervously when I'm overwhelmed. Today, I'm a competent speaker, some would even say skilled, but none of it happened by accident.

I've hired acting and speech coaches, read books, and volunteered to speak at dozens of places and events, from schools and conferences to television news programs and, eventually, TEDx stages.

Along the way, I performed in community theater productions, participated in open mics at stand-up comedy clubs, and read short stories at literary events. This was all painfully uncomfortable for me, but public speaking is the backbone of what I do, so it was worth it. Additionally, honing your public speaking skills can give you a tremendous advantage, since most teachers don't bother.

If you're like I was and know you need to improve your speaking, I'd recommend you consider Toastmasters, a member-led organization where you can meet with peers and develop and refine a formal talk. You might also consider joining an improv group or theater group, or even hiring a speaking coach.

> **Q:** If you really wanted to improve your speaking skills in the next three months, what could you do outside of teaching yoga that could take you to the next level? Acting? Improv? Voice lessons?

SOFTWARE AND TECHNOLOGY SKILLS

To stay competitive as a yoga teacher, you must be tech positive and willing to learn new things. Whether you're doing a live class on Zoom or hosting a video session on social media, you need to embrace technology. Most of my early teachers shunned the digital yoga revolution, and unfortunately, most are largely forgotten and struggle to pay their bills today.

There is a huge technological divide right now, and you don't want to be stuck on the wrong side. Pattabhi Jois and BKS Iyengar used to practice yoga on rugs; now we have sticky mats and we're all happier. Sticky yoga mats are technology. Yoga writing used to be exclusively limited to books. Today, we use blogs, websites, and social media even more than books. This allows for more writing, more teaching, and more learning. Books are great; the web is great. Technology is here to stay. It's not good or bad; it's just here. Accept it.

The most common technological mistake I see teachers make is trying to run their entire businesses from their phones. If you want to grow your business, you'll need a laptop or desktop computer. I don't care about the brand or the model, but you need a real keyboard and a screen or you'll never be productive enough to earn a decent living. I don't care how fast you think you are on your phone; you're five times faster on a computer.

Next, you need to master whatever tools you're using regularly. If you're teaching on Zoom, study it. If you're using YouTube to publish videos, learn the platform. If you can learn sun salute B, you can learn how to use email, social media, and basic web services.

I have a friend who has taught yoga for over thirty years. He is loved by students on three continents, and yet, he hasn't managed to email them in nearly a decade. Why? He didn't bother to learn how to use email management services such as Mailchimp, and when everyone switched to Gmail, he stuck with his Yahoo address from 1998.

I'm not mocking him—we all do this to some extent. We hold on to the past as if it were somehow better. We get so frustrated by the pace at which things are moving that we want to throw up our hands and say, "Forget it!" but that's not helpful.

If your computer skills are lacking, YouTube will be your best teacher. There are tutorials on how to use Instagram and Zoom but also on how to select a computer, how to set up keyboard shortcuts, and how to organize your desktop. Don't be embarrassed by what you don't know. Despite the fact that I'm extremely tech positive, I hardly know anything—but I know how to look, and I educate myself constantly. Use your phone less, use your computer more, and start watching tutorials. You've got this.

ORGANIZATIONAL SKILLS

The world is cruel to the disorganized. If you miss a class due to schedule mix-ups, you might not get another call…ever. If you can't find the PDF file for the workshop handout, your students might give you one- and two-star reviews when you should be getting fours and fives. The first step toward organization is acknowledging that it's important. The second step is to remember that how you organize anything is usually how you organize everything. If your sock drawer is a mess, your computer filing system is probably in the same state of disarray.

Organization is challenging because it's never ending. The moment you get your email inbox emptied, your taxes are due. You finally get your accounts balanced, and suddenly you realize your insurance has expired.

Drop the guilt, put your chin down, and get to work. Start with your sock drawer, move on to your computer, and slowly but surely get your ducks in a row. It's important.

Everyone has different systems that work for them. Some (like me) use checklists, some hire help, others follow books like David Allen's *Getting Things Done*. Do whatever works for you, and know that the more organized you become, the more students you'll impact, and the more money and peace you'll obtain.

Q: Do you have a digital calendar where you plan your days, weeks, and months? Do you have an email list management system like Mailchimp where you can broadcast announcements to your students? Is your online profile updated, or do you have classes on your calendar from last month or last year?

FINANCIAL LITERACY SKILLS

Did you know that almost every yoga teacher I work with earns more money the moment they start tracking and logging their income and expenses? This is because many of your current expenses can be written off as business expenses for tax purposes, and I guarantee that you have outstanding invoices owed to you by studios or clients who simply forgot to pay.

When I encourage teachers to collect outstanding income, most uncover around $1,000. I had one teacher who realized they were due a tax refund of $4,123! Truthfully, my finances used to be a mess. I used to send all my bills to an accountant and figured everything would be fine, but it's never that simple. I was so sloppy with my billing that I once accidentally forgot to collect a $40,000 invoice for eighteen months! To add to the pain, I owed over half that money to a colleague.

I looked like a fool, I'd been out a huge chunk of money, and I lost the trust of the people on both sides of the transaction. Most yoga teachers don't like numbers or accounting, but clearly, you're reading this book because you want to see the numbers in your bank account go up, right?

Financial literacy might not be fun, but it's very profitable. If you don't have a system, start now by simply keeping an Excel or Google Sheet with your money earned (revenue) and money spent (expenses). Eventually, you'll move to a system like QuickBooks or Xero, but keep it simple and just start with a ledger.

One of the best teachers I'd recommend to learn about financial literacy is Remit Sethi. He's a bestselling author, but even if you don't buy his books, his website (www. iwillteachyoutoberich.com) is loaded with free resources to help you get your finances in order.

Shortcut to Success

Years ago, a couple in their forties graduated from one of my teacher training programs. Both of them had been practicing for about one year, so they were brand-new teachers with 200-hour certificates. They both felt impostor syndrome biting and didn't think they were ready to move forward in their careers without further education.

They came to me wanting to train for a 500-hour certificate so they could add to their résumés before they took the next steps toward their ultimate dream of opening a studio. I encouraged them to forget about opening a studio and pursuing further certifications and instead start teaching as quickly as possible.

Initially, they were flustered and disappointed with my response, but to their credit, they listened. They quickly partnered with a local gym to use a room within the facility. They didn't invest any money or waste time building a brick-and-mortar studio, and they certainly didn't waste time pursuing further education when what they really needed to do was use their existing skills and knowledge.

I was delighted to learn that their initial classes were capping out at twenty-eight people and that soon they were at full capacity.

Before long, the two of them maxed out their own teaching schedules and recruited more teachers. To the best of my knowledge, both teachers have continued with advanced training and gained more certifications, which is great, but the continuing education is not what unlocked their financial or teaching success. That was due to the fact that despite that initial imposter syndrome, they moved forward anyway.

CHAPTER III

Positioning for Success

M ost of my life, I had only two or three friends at a time. Once I started teaching yoga, I suddenly knew dozens of people with whom I spent hours moving, breathing, and sweating together in classes. Outside of yoga, there were constant dinners, art openings, and picnics. My social circle suddenly exploded. As an introvert, small talk is difficult for me, so meeting all those new people was exhausting.

Again and again, people at these events asked me, "What do you do?" I hated this question because when I said I was a yoga teacher, they either changed the subject or made jokes about levitation. It was so predictable that to get past the stereotypes, I started experimenting with different answers.

When someone asked me, "So what do you do?" my new reply went like this: "You know how people want to get fit, but they're bored with gym workouts?"

The person usually nodded their head. "I teach a Power Yoga class where you get an amazing workout, but you do it with a group of friends so it's more fun. And since it's a skill-based practice, you actually see yourself building strength and flexibility instead of just running on a treadmill."

What happened next really surprised me. People's eyes got brighter. They leaned in close and started asking questions. They started sharing stories about their back or knee problems. They asked whether Power Yoga was as effective as going to the gym, or was it just stretching? Most surprising of all, these new acquaintances started attending my classes. Just like that, I went from being the freaky new age weirdo at the party to being a Power Yoga instructor whose classes everyone wanted to join.

I had accidentally stumbled on the power of positioning, and this insight completely transformed my career. In this chapter, you'll learn how unique, value-based positioning is the single most effective way to grow your business as a teacher.

The Power of a Unique Teaching Position (UTP)

In every industry, specialists earn more money, attract more clients, and add value to their market, instead of competing. You can see examples of this all around you. A general hair stylist competes with everyone else in town, whereas the stylist who focuses on wedding updos can charge two to five times as much as her peers, while operating with little or no competition.

A general medical doctor will often earn 50 percent less than their dermatologist or podiatrist peers, all with a similar level of education, while servicing the same clients and often while working in the same facility. In just about every market, specialized services are valued more highly than general ones.

Here's how this dynamic works in yoga. Let's imagine you want to join a weekend workshop, and you need to decide between two simultaneous offerings. One workshop is called something general, like *Introduction to Hatha Yoga*. The second workshop is called *Hamstring Freedom*. Which workshop will attract more students? Which workshop will generate more revenue? Which workshop would you sign up for?

The hamstring workshop will be more successful because it has a clear, value-added positioning, and it's obvious what is being offered. The Hatha Yoga workshop could be amazing, but almost no one wakes up on a Saturday morning and thinks, "Oh, I need some Hatha Yoga in my life!" Many of us, however, wake up thinking, "My hamstrings are so tight! I better do something, or I'm bound to get injured soon."

Party Conversation Exercise (fill in the blanks)

Imagine you're at a picnic with a bunch of people you don't know, and the question inevitably comes up: "So what do you do?"

Using your list of possible teaching positions, plug them into the sentence below. See how they feel. See which ones get you excited. Make a note of the winners and scrap the teaching positions that don't feel like a good fit for you and your potential students.

Fill in the blanks here: "You know how people struggle with _____ [specific problem]? I teach yoga for _____ [specific solution-oriented class]."

Strong Positioning = Problem + Solution

As a yoga teacher, you are a service provider, and the service business revolves around problems and solutions. Nothing else. Do you have a leaky pipe? A plumber can help. Do you have a tax issue? Okay, call a certified public accountant. Suffering from a toothache? Call the dentist.

In my early years of teaching, I didn't realize that the plumber, the accountant, the local dentist, and I were *all* in the service industry, doing our best to solve problems for our clients.

As a service provider, always remember that you are not your ideal client. What do I mean by this? You and I are yoga people. We love yoga for yoga's sake. For me, yoga is an obsession. I've tried every style of yoga I could find. I buy obscure yoga books just because. I read yoga history, study anatomy in my spare time, and watch YouTube videos about yoga on my off days. That's what yoga people do.

My clients are not like me, and neither are yours.

For most of our clients, their interest in yoga manifests differently. On a random Tuesday, they wake up feeling less than excited about their health and think, "Should I go to yoga tonight after work?" The decision-making process that follows has nothing to do with alignment or their breath. They're not thinking about mastering half-moon pose or getting deeper in a backbend. They're thinking about how badly they slept last night, how annoying their lower back pain is, or how long it's been since they put their energy into anything except work and family.

If you were to speak to this potential client as though they were a yoga insider, sharing tips on wrist alignment or feet placement in a squat, you would instantly alienate them. As a service provider, your job is to meet that potential student where they're at on that Tuesday morning and speak to them about their unique life challenges: knee pain, stress, overwhelm, weight gain, social isolation, lack of purpose, or whatever else might be going on for them.

A strong teaching position, by definition, means your classes won't be for everyone—and that's okay. If you specialize in pelvic floor rehab, for example, the stressed-out office worker trying to lose ten pounds might not be interested in your work. This is not a problem. You'll be a magnet for some and repellent for others. Stay focused. If you try to be all things to all people, you'll end up with the worst-paying, most poorly attended classes in town. Think about problems, do your best to offer yoga-based solutions, and watch your teaching business grow.

Your UTP May Be Right Under Your Nose

If you're struggling with your UTP, that's a good sign. This process is important and worthy of some struggle. Often, your unique position is hiding in plain sight.

I had a trainee named Antonia who was frustrated and stuck, unable to figure out what to specialize in. She loved yoga and was a passionate student, but she just couldn't see herself solving specific problems for her clients. Her local classes at the YMCA were called Yoga Level I. If there were ever a generalist class, hers was it.

She kept telling me, "My class is for everyone! Everyone can benefit!" But the numbers told a different story. She averaged just two to three students per session, so clearly, something was off. I pushed her to dig deeper into her past skills and experiences, and suddenly, she had a breakthrough!

Before yoga, Antonia had worked as an in-home nurse, and she'd become the go-to person on her team for helping clients with colon cancer learn how to navigate life with a colostomy bag. She shared this reluctantly and seemed a little embarrassed. I pressed her for details. As it turns out, when people have colostomy bags, many are apprehensive to do any form of exercise at all because of the self-consciousness that arises when you're carrying around a bag of your own excrement. At the same time, these clients need to exercise more than anyone.

Suddenly, Antonia thought, "What about yoga for people with colostomy bags?" I think she was expecting a laugh, but instead, I did a quick Google search. At the time, there was literally no one on planet Earth offering anything like this. There it was! Her UTP.

Antonia opted for online classes since she thought students would be more comfortable. She also decided on small-group classes since she knew these clients would appreciate a supportive community of people experiencing the same health challenges.

And what about marketing? Antonia found Facebook groups, Subreddits, and online forums dedicated exclusively to living with colon cancer. Could it be this simple? Sometimes, yes! Antonia had a unique skillset that she combined with her general knowledge of yoga to create a truly specialized yoga class. Almost no one in the world was as qualified as she was to teach this class, so Antonia literally owned this category.

Her classes immediately tripled in size, and she charged her students twice as much as the rates at her local studio for her group classes. Since she was working for herself now, outside the studio setting, her actual per-class income went up by seven times. That is the power of specialization.

Unique Teaching Position Options to Consider

Problem: Scoliosis
Solution: Yoga for Scoliosis
Unique Teaching Position: Yoga for Scoliosis will help you reduce pain, increase mobility, and live your most-active-possible life.

Problem: Insomnia
Solution: Yoga for Sleep
Unique Teaching Position: Yoga for Sleep helps you fall asleep faster and improve the quality of your sleep using breathwork and mindfulness practices.

Problem: Overweight
Solution: Yoga for Weight Loss
Unique Teaching Position: Yoga for Weight Loss takes a mind-body approach to fitness by reducing stress, balancing hormones, and creating emotional balance for change.

Problem: Knee pain
Solution: Yoga for Strong Knees
Unique Teaching Position: Yoga for Strong Knees is a class focused on strengthening the supporting muscles of the knees and developing full range of motion to alleviate and even eliminate many types of knee pain.

Problem: Prolapse and incontinence postpartum
Solution: Postpartum Yoga
Unique Teaching Position: Postpartum Yoga helps new moms restore their pelvic floor, reverse prolapse, and end incontinence forever.

Problem: Bad posture
Solution: Yoga for Better Posture
Unique Teaching Position: Yoga for Better Posture builds strength of the posterior chain and develops full-body flexibility so you can stand up straight, care for your joints, and avoid injuries.

Problem: Post-traumatic stress disorder (PTSD)
Solution: Trauma Release Yoga
Unique Teaching Position: Trauma Release Yoga combines cognitive behavioral therapy with traditional yoga practices to create a safe and supportive space for change.

Problem: Alcohol addiction
Solution: Sober Yoga
Unique Teaching Position: Sober Yoga is a supportive group class that teaches you to channel your addictive energy into a positive, healing journey back home.

Problem: Lonely expatriates living in Paris
Solution: Yoga in English
Unique Teaching Position: Get in shape and build strength and flexibility as part of Paris's only Yoga for English Speakers class on Saturday mornings.

Problem: Poor body image
Solution: Body Positive Yoga
Unique Teaching Position: Body Positive Yoga is a vinyasa flow class for all sizes and shapes with personalized modifications and support.

Problem: Very few men in most yoga classes
Solution: Yoga for Men
Unique Teaching Position: Yoga for Men is a strong, supportive group of guys who get together on Tuesday and Thursday evenings to sweat it out on the mat.

Problem: Low self-esteem
Solution: Yoga for Personal Power
Unique Teaching Position: Yoga for Personal Power uses progressive yoga practices to build your mental and physical confidence pose by pose, class by class, in a supportive environment.

Problem: Cancer recovery
Solution: Yoga for Cancer Survivors
Unique Teaching Position: Yoga for Cancer Survivors is a supportive class for those healing from cancer and actively rebuilding their physical and mental strength.

Problem: Midlife crisis
Solution: Yoga for 50+
Unique Teaching Position: Yoga for the 2nd Half is a dynamic, progressive class for people over fifty who want to squeeze every last drop out of life.

Problem: Unable to walk/stand
Solution: Chair Yoga
Unique Teaching Position: Chair Yoga is a dynamic mind-body-breath practice that will improve circulation, mobilize your joints, and leave you feeling light and energized.

Problem: No time
Solution: New Mom Online Yoga
Unique Teaching Position: New Mom Online Yoga is a live, late-night class specifically for new moms who just don't have time to get to the studio.

Specialization Is *Not* Limitation

Teachers often worry they'll become pigeonholed by focusing so narrowly on a unique teaching position. You love so many different things in yoga, and your interests span the globe, right? Me too, but don't worry, specialization doesn't restrict you. You don't have to limit yourself to one unique teaching position, but you do need to focus on just one at a time.

Early on, I specialized in athletic Power Yoga classes as an alternative for bored gym-goers who still wanted a great workout. Later, I specialized in yoga for flexibility, breathwork for deep sleep and relaxation, and yoga for weight loss.

Start by focusing on just one unique teaching position. Our goal is to dig deep wells of expertise, so it's not possible to develop master-level knowledge in dozens of areas. Over the course of your career, you will likely develop two to five unique positions, and this will create a rich and diverse teaching life.

Your Past Often Informs Your Specialty

Ben was an occupational therapist who discovered yoga in his fifties. As a therapist, he mostly helped older people recover from slips, falls, and broken bones. Ben's clients regained the ability to perform everyday tasks: getting in and out of chairs, using the stairs, and entering and exiting vehicles.

As a student, Ben was passionate about hot yoga. He loved how physically demanding it was, and how he finished class in a puddle of his own sweat. He loved the practice so much that he'd trained and was certified as a hot yoga instructor. Ben's clients were in active recovery from injuries, so he never considered them as potential students for hot-style yoga.

I reminded Ben what I'll remind you again here: *you* are not your ideal client.

The fact that Ben loved an extremely demanding style of yoga didn't in any way exclude him from offering a gentler, less-aggressive practice to his occupational therapy clients—and that's exactly what he did. Instead of leaving occupational therapy to teach hot yoga as he had originally planned, he unlocked an entirely new job within his job, teaching what he called Yoga for Life Skills, a safe and slow series custom sequenced for his clients' needs, practiced with props and support.

Five-Minute Writing Assignment

Now it's your turn to discover your unique teaching position. Take five minutes and write down the skills or past experiences that could potentially position you as the obvious choice for a particular group of students. Don't overthink or analyze for now—just write.

Questions to consider:
- Have you had a unique past work experience?
- Did you use yoga to manage _____ condition?
- Have you had back, neck, knee, or shoulder problems?
- Do you speak multiple languages?
- Are you qualified in other modalities that might pair well with yoga?
- Do you have access to a unique social group or corporate group?
- Are you affiliated with a church or community organization?
- What makes you different as a teacher and person?
- What problems could you best help your students solve?

Spirituality Is Not for Sale

Many yoga teachers throw a spiritual solution at just about any problem by default. Overwhelmed with stress? You need to balance your chakras. Having back pain? You probably have emotional blocks from past trauma. Suffering from chronic fatigue? You should awaken your Kundalini energy. This type of esoteric positioning is common in yoga, but I'd encourage you to avoid it completely.

In business, you can sell either products or services, and since spirituality doesn't fit into either of those categories, it's best not to monetize it at all. I'm not saying don't teach or preach spirituality if that's your thing; I'm simply saying don't sell it. Selling spirituality is lazy at best and unethical at worst. Instead, sell solutions to problems using yoga as a tool.

Specializing in Yoga for Eating Disorders

Mimi taught Vinyasa Yoga in London and struggled to find a steady clientele. Her classes were well liked but not loved. She had some steady clients, but things were not growing. This same story plays out every day in studios across the world.

Mimi originally discovered yoga as part of her own healing journey from a battle with anorexia. Yoga had helped her learn to love her body, but just as importantly, she had found a supportive group of people who were health focused and body positive. As she shared her story with me, a light bulb went off. Yoga for Eating Disorders? There it was!

How many teenagers in London were suffering alone with eating disorders? Tens of thousands, maybe more. And how many yoga teachers were offering classes targeting this group? At that time, there was literally no one offering anything like this. Here's why this is so exciting: nearly nine million people live in London. Mimi had virtually no competition, there was a huge demand, she could charge higher rates, and her work was extremely rewarding.

Mimi was able to leverage her experiences to create a truly unique and value-added class operating completely outside the normal yoga scene. Her classes were coordinated through a local teen support center, students signed up (and paid) in advance for a twelve-week program, and Mimi increased her income by 180 percent pretty much overnight.

CHAPTER IV

You + Your Community = Business

Sara taught the most popular class at my old studio. She was a newer teacher, and her sequences were good but not remarkable. What made Sara's classes so popular was her ability to create community. For me, as an introvert, it was amazing to watch and learn.

Sara remembered everyone's names and always shared encouraging tips and suggestions with students. I'd see her on the floor in the lobby, demonstrating poses before class and answering questions afterwards, always fully present. The best part is, she did all of this naturally; none of it was performative or forced.

Students showed up early and lingered long after classes to talk. They waited for Sara, but just as often, they waited for each other. Sara wasn't a guru figure; she was a master at social connection. People felt comfortable with her and with themselves, so they opened up to one another.

The busiest classes were Tuesday and Thursday evenings, and more than once, we had to turn people away. We sold out! From my perspective, as a studio owner, it was all very exciting. Sara was glowing, the students were happy, and the overflowing classes were great for my business.

And then, just as quickly as it started, it ended.

A studio around the corner offered Sara an ownership stake and a lead teacher role. It sounded like a great opportunity, and I don't blame her for saying yes. What happened next, however, shocked me and forever changed how I think about the business of yoga.

Over 80 percent of Sara's regular students canceled their memberships and walked out the door. Why? They didn't care about my studio, all the money I'd invested, my logo, or my carefully chosen color scheme. Why would they? Their connection was to Sara. It stands to reason that they followed her out the door, down the street, and to her new classes with my competitor.

At the time, it was a huge blow to me personally and professionally. I'd dumped my life savings into this studio. I felt a sense of ownership over the classes, the students, and to some extent, even the team. Like many small business owners, I was naive and didn't understand where the real business assets were hidden. My studios themselves had virtually no value. All the value came from the teachers and the communities that developed around them.

Parallels to the Music Industry

In the music business, no one cares which label publishes their favorite artists. In the yoga world, the only items of value are a teacher and their community. I refer to these two assets as *you* and *your community*.

You includes all your skills and abilities, experiences, and knowledge.

Your community includes all the people who know, like, and trust you. This includes the students who come to your classes, the employers you work for, and the business partners you collaborate with.

As often happens, the studio Sara joined went out of business six months later, and she returned asking for her old job back. I didn't have any bad feelings toward her, but I said no because I could see that Sara was destined for bigger things, and she didn't need me or the studio to get there.

As I mentioned, Sara was an amazing community builder, but her teaching skills needed development. Fortunately, she met a senior teacher who took her under her wing and they co-taught together for the next six months. In the short term, Sara struggled financially since she was working as a teaching assistant, but she was investing in herself—her *you* asset—and it paid off. Her teaching skills went from average to exceptional in a hurry.

Today, Sara's teaching specialty focuses on arm balances, flying transitions, and acrobatic-style yoga. Her unique teaching position is crystal clear, and all on her own, she has built a wonderful business for herself that includes private clients, partner yoga sessions, retreats, and studio workshops. I'm certain that her income has more than tripled since she worked for me, and I've been cheering her on from afar ever since.

Beware of the Biznaz Trap

As soon as I say "yoga" and "business" in the same sentence, it conjures up images of local studios, T-shirts, reception desks, websites, logos, and taglines. Every week, teachers and studio owners around the world ask for help with branding, choosing the best yoga mats, or finding the ideal flooring for a commercial venue.

These topics are fun to discuss, and they feel important—but they are not. Collectively, I like to refer to these peripheral business activities as *Biznaz*.

Have you ever been to a shopping mall and heard a song that sounded like the Beatles, only it wasn't? Perhaps you've heard an instrumental version of *Let It Be*, barely audible, playing in a hotel elevator? That's called Muzak, and it's been around for nearly one hundred years. Muzak sounds like your favorite artist, but it isn't. It's designed to fill the dead air of retail businesses. Biznaz is the same. It seems like important business-building tasks, vital to your success, but in fact, it's mostly filler.

Biznaz is the background music of business. Yes, sometimes you do need it to create a vibe, but it's not what your students value or pay for, and ultimately, it'll be ignored.

Why do so many business coaches focus on personal branding, mission statements, color schemes, and logo design as a crucial part of entrepreneurship? They teach this because it's fun and doesn't require the difficult work of improving yourself as a service provider and building an actual community of raving fans.

Anyone can spend an afternoon picking out yoga props and essential oils for the bathrooms, but very few people will sit down and dedicate themselves to real business growth. *You* and *your community* are the only assets that matter. These two assets drive revenue, and they are the only things you'll be known and remembered for.

If anyone needs to hear this message, it's me. As I'm writing, I'm staring at a human-size sticker of my logo stuck to the window of my office. There's a rack of branded T-shirts in the corner, and I have my company's five core values mounted on a wooden board. At one point, I was so confused about the yoga business that I ordered five hundred temporary tattoos of my YOGABODY logo to give to students. Aside from my five-year-old son, no one used a single tattoo.

Looking back, it's embarrassing how much time and money I wasted.

If I could, I'd rewind the clock, skip most of the Biznaz activities, and invest instead in myself and my community. I know dozens of teachers who have done just that and were able to establish successful businesses faster than I did. Many have terrible websites, have no logo, and have never bothered to formally incorporate their businesses. I'm not advocating sloppy business practices, but the goal of this chapter is to help you separate the signal from the noise and focus on the highest-leverage activities.

YOU: Your Knowledge, Skills, and Experiences

When you think about actively building your business, you must start by building yourself up: your knowledge, your skills, and your experiences. This includes all the things related to your style of yoga and your personal practice, of course, but it also includes all the soft and hard skills covered in Chapter III.

A common mistake is to assume that yoga practice itself constitutes professional development. You should be a committed student of yoga, yes, but also a student of leadership, public speaking, organization, and problem solving. I know many amazing yoga practitioners with decades of experience who are unfit to lead a group in anything. You don't get paid to perform postures; you get paid to teach, and the skills required to do this at a high level require deliberate practice too.

The second common mistake is to assume that a busy teaching schedule will automatically improve your skills. Maybe yes, maybe not. Without intention and planning, many teachers plateau very quickly and spin their wheels toward inevitable burnout. When you're done teaching for the day, think of your work as half done. The second half of your work must be focused on professional growth.

How Are Your Professional Skills?

On a scale of one to ten, how would you rate your skill level in the following areas?

Yoga Skills
- Yoga practice competency
- Expertise in your yoga specialties
- Anatomy and biomechanics
- Injuries, adjustments, modifications
- Sequencing

Soft and Hard Skills
- Leadership
- Communication
- Interpersonal skills
- Motivational skills
- Teamwork
- Problem solving
- Public speaking
- Software and technology

Any skill that you ranked five or less, add to your "to improve" list right away. Although this can seem overwhelming at first, remember, almost none of your colleagues are actively bettering themselves, and just a few short months from now, you'll begin to stand out as a thought leader in your market.

HOW TO BUILD YOURSELF UP

Author G. K. Chesterton said, "If a thing is worth doing, it is worth doing badly." I agree but would add the caveat "at first." Anything worth doing is worth doing badly *at first*.

If you need to improve your public speaking, offer a free talk on injuries and yoga at your local studio this month. Stumble forward, drag yourself through the process of preparing a talk, and embrace the fact that your first efforts will be lackluster.

Are your hips tight? Does that limit what you can teach and hurt your confidence? Commit to a hundred-day program of daily hip openers before bed. Are your organizational skills horrible? Do you have stacks of papers in the drawer and unanswered emails from months ago? Sit down and set some new rules for yourself. Sort through the papers; whittle down those emails.

Are you struggling to learn students' names in classes? Decide today to address this problem, no matter what it takes. Every class, from now on, say at least three students' names aloud while teaching. Greet people by name before and after sessions. Review your attendance list after class and you'll very quickly see the impact of this personal touch.

Nothing I'm suggesting is an overnight fix. You should expect to slip up and go back to your old patterns many times. That's okay. Commit to the process, continue to work on yourself proactively, and your *you* asset will grow steadily over time.

As I'm writing this, I'm actively learning to use YouTube better from a technical standpoint. I'm also working on sequences to improve dorsiflexion range both for me and for my students. Last, my social media inboxes are overflowing and poorly managed—that needs fixing. By the time you read this, I'll have made huge strides forward in all three of these areas and will surely be working on other areas of professional growth.

How Strong Is Your Community?

Your community consists of the students you serve: people who know, like, and trust you. This also includes employers and potential business partners. Many teachers assume that their goal is to amass a huge social media following, but there are plenty of teachers whose communities consist of text message groups, email lists, handwritten notebooks, or some combination of all of these.

Before we explore strategies to grow your community, let's first quantify your total reach today so we can track your progress over time. On a piece of paper, write down your total audience size in each of the community channels listed below. If you have contacts on another platform, feel free to add more channels to the list.

How many?
- Email contacts
- Phone contacts
- Messaging app contacts
- Social media followers
- Meetup.com groups
- Other social groups

Let's use the total number as your total community size as of today. No matter how big or small, ask yourself this: What would happen if I announced a new class or workshop? How many people might be interested?

My community started with a clipboard and a blank sheet of paper. After classes one day, I announced that I was collecting emails for future events and invited people to write down their details. It wasn't elegant or automated, but it was enough. Thirty-two people wrote their names down, and a month later, I announced my first yoga retreat in Thailand. Six people from that initial list signed up to attend the retreat, and I was officially in business.

I started in the pre-social media world with just a clipboard with thirty-two names. You can do this too, and I wouldn't be surprised if you can do it better. Maybe you have only seventy-three followers on Instagram or twelve telephone contacts from past students. Maybe you're a member of a local fitness group or you have a small Facebook page. Whatever assets you have, big or small, tally them up, and get to work.

How to Grow Your Community

Communities are based on relationships, and in the business of yoga, we want to build student-teacher relationships. It'll come as no surprise when I tell you that the best way to build these connections is via personal conversation or published materials that are 100 percent in line with what you do. If your specialty is postpartum care, share your research, create video tutorials for new moms, and message directly with students when questions come in.

Build your community online, off-line, in person, through video classes, via text messages, via email, or through whatever means students reach out to you. Connections happen in class, but they also happen online and in messages. Don't discriminate, just connect, and serve; you'll see the impact very quickly.

I ran monthlong courses in Thailand for fourteen years, and when I asked students why they chose to come to my courses, one of the top answers was, "You were the only one that answered my emails." Students would email five course directors; I was the one who answered promptly and professionally, and they chose me for that reason alone.

As you build your community, you'll make friends and colleagues along the way, but that's a happy accident. Your focus should always be on adding value to your students' lives by sharing and teaching within your area of expertise.

On social media, it's easy to get lost in vanity metrics such as the number of likes, comments, or follows on your accounts. This is a mistake. I've had silly yoga videos go viral and reach millions of people in a span of weeks. I was excited at first, but in the end, it did nothing for my business or my community. Today, I couldn't care less how many followers I have, but I'm laser-focused on constant and continuous community building.

Today, when I open my email, my phone, or my social media apps, I'll find dozens of questions from real people all around the world with back pain, flexibility problems, breathing challenges, and more. Instead of chasing viral videos, I now invest my time directly into my people. I send email replies and voice messages to every single person who writes. Sometimes I'm a day or two behind with the volume of inbound, but I make it a priority to build my community through real connections daily.

Growth Never Stops

As the saying goes, "When you're green, you grow, and when you're ripe, you rot." In yoga teaching, this has proven true time and time again. Today, I invest more in myself and my community than ever before in my career.

I'm constantly reading new books, hiring coaches, and growing professionally to improve my *you* asset. Compared to many of my peers, I've done very well, but compared to where I'd like to be, I have decades of learning to go.

My colleagues often criticize me for answering so many questions every single day. What they fail to realize is that the reason I am so successful is because I never stop serving and growing my community. Communities are built through real people and real interactions, online and off-line, and I invest in that asset each day. You should too.

Energetic Equity vs. Real Estate Equity

I had a client named Bruce who owned a struggling yoga studio. He also owned the property where the studio operated. More accurately, he had a twenty-five-year mortgage. Like at most small studios, Bruce was the owner, operator, manager, and head teacher. Of twelve weekly classes, he taught ten himself.

He averaged six to eight students per class, and the studio generated about $3,000 per month in revenue. At the end of each month, after paying the mortgage, taxes, electric bills, and his extra teacher's salary, Bruce was left with about $400, which works out to a measly $10 per class—not even enough to survive.

"But I own the building!" Bruce told me. He was excited that in just twenty-three years' time, this 2,000-square-foot space in a strip mall would be his, owned free and clear. Unfortunately, there were two major problems. First, buying commercial real estate in strip malls is an entirely different business from teaching yoga. Second, the real estate market was upside down at the time, so Bruce's property was worth less than what he'd paid for it.

Bruce initially contacted me to help fix his studio business, but the studio was a lost cause. The math just didn't work out. Luckily, we quickly uncovered a new opportunity. Bruce was a skilled teacher and had built up a very strong community. Over time, a community grows in equity, just like a piece of real estate. I like to call this energetic equity.

Energetic equity is best understood as the long-term trust, connection, and loyalty that you earn through service to your clients. Bruce had been teaching nonstop for two years, and he'd never offered anything except his daily group classes. He'd connected with a lot of students, many of whom were excited to take more classes with him.

I suggested Bruce host a five-day retreat in Mexico at a resort he knew from past travels. With a couple of phone calls, Bruce had a tentative group reservation, and he quickly crafted a promotional email to his list. *New Year, New You in Tulum* was the name of his event. By the end of the week, he had sold out all twenty-two spots. Within ten days, he had made a $4,000 profit.

Was Bruce's studio worth it in the end? No, the studio was a money pit and a time suck. The real value was hiding in Bruce's community, and he could have and should have built that asset while working for someone else, earning a decent living along the way. By leveraging his energetic equity, Bruce went from earning $400 a month to $4,000.

Old-school ideas about business are very hard to shake, and many people assume that brick-and-mortar locations are the key to success. I still sometimes need to remind myself where to put my energy, because the siren song of Biznaz is so strong. The rewards of growing both *you* and *your community*, however, are more than worth the effort. If you can ruthlessly focus on these two assets, you'll uncover hidden opportunities, more income, and more rewarding work, just like Bruce did.

CHAPTER V

Define Your Success

During my second year as a teacher, I took an overnight camping trip with a group of colleagues. The idea was to network and practice together. One evening, we sat around a campfire and took turns sharing our goals for the upcoming year.

One woman wanted to master a handstand pose in the middle of the room. Another dreamed of walking gracefully in high heels. A third teacher told us he was saving up for a yoga vacation in Bali. When it was my turn, I announced self-consciously that I wanted to start my own yoga business, feeling as though I was grandstanding to share such a lofty goal. I was the greenest of the bunch, and I could see the others holding back smiles of doubt.

That evening, a couple of things became clear. First, I needed to upgrade my peer group. I loved practicing and teaching with these new friends, but their ideal future was not aligned with mine. Second, I realized that although I was ambitious, I didn't know what I really wanted—I just knew I wanted more. I was living week to week and wanted to build something bigger. But what? And where? And why?

Fast forward to nine months later. I'd opened my first studio— the only yoga business idea I could come up with at the time. Finally, I was able to set my own schedule, make all the important decisions, and even earn more money. The only problem was that I felt like a failure.

That first year in business, I worked seventy hours per week, wrestled with endless responsibilities, and blew up the most important relationship in my life. I was teaching, hiring, advertising, managing the website, and so much more. The studio was a financial success from day one, but it never became a personal success. I was lonely, burned out, and lost.

If I could go back to that campfire and reshare my goals, I would be much more specific in defining success on my own terms. I wanted a family, financial stability, and a demanding but manageable workload. In this chapter, my goal is to help you avoid the pitfalls of ambiguous aspirations and create specific you-centric goals that will lead toward your ideal outcome.

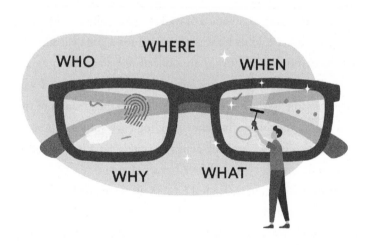

The Five Ws

To achieve your goals, you first need a clear understanding of what they are and why they matter to you. There are five questions you need to answer before you can define success: why, who, what, where, and when. Once you're able to clearly answer each of these five questions, you'll increase your odds of achieving success rapidly, and you'll be happier with your results.

WHY

Business can be very challenging, so you must keep your deepest motivation at the top of your mind throughout the journey. Friedrich Nietzsche once said, "He who has a why to live for can bear almost any how." Why do you want to do this? What is your strongest motivator right now?

When I first started teaching yoga, my why was travel. I thought teaching would enable me to explore the world, and I was right! When I decided to start my own business, my why changed. I wanted financial freedom, control over my career, and ultimately, the ability to impact more lives through my work. Those are lofty reasons why I do what I do, and to be honest, I'm still working on them to this day. What about you? What is the proverbial carrot you're chasing?

- Why are you committing to the life of a teacher?
- Aside from earning a living, what else motivates you?
- What are your personal needs and wants right now?
- What aspects of yoga teaching provide meaning and significance for you?
- What contribution or "body of work" would fulfill you?

Before reading further, take some time to explore the reasons why you do what you do. Perhaps your biggest motivation right now is to quit a dead-end job that's eating your soul. That's great. Or maybe your *why* is to empower stressed-out office workers with the tools of yoga to deal with overwhelm and anxiety. Also great. Whether your *why* is humble or grandiose, make sure it's honest and true for you right now.

WHO

In the previous chapter, we defined your community as the students you serve and those you work with. As part of defining success, I'd like you to think through exactly what types of people you'd like to be surrounded by.

- What types of clients would you like to have?
- What types of colleagues would inspire you?
- Who, if anyone, would you like to work for?
- What types of people are you excited to work with?
- Who would you like to avoid completely?

Many teachers say they want to work with everyone possible. This is a lovely thought, but it's just not true. I could tell you that I want to work with professional athletes, for example, but I don't have a background in athletics, and I don't know the first thing about sports. Athletes are not on my *who* list.

Since my own yoga journey is one of personal transformation, I love working with people in a transitional phase of life. My ideal client is new to yoga and often new to mind-body practices altogether. My *who* list consists of beginners, people experiencing a health crisis, and students looking for meaning and purpose through practice.

Remember, we're all molded by those around us—clients, colleagues, and employers—so choose wisely and give yourself permission to be picky about who will enter your new world.

WHAT

Yoga means many different things to different people, so let's use this opportunity to specifically define *what* you'll offer. To give you a real-world example, let me share with you my current list. Currently, I teach yoga for breathing, yoga for flexibility, and Yoga Trapeze. I mostly teach group classes, and I tend to focus on trainings or intensive practice workshops. I've also worked as a keynote speaker and corporate wellness trainer for large companies.

- What style of yoga will you teach?
- What format will you teach in? (privately, group, workshops)
- Are there teachers or books you'll use to anchor your instruction?

If you need additional clarity, go back to Chapter III. Think about problems and solutions, and remember that as a yoga teacher, you're a service provider. First and foremost, you should be in service to your clients' needs.

WHERE

First, let's think about teaching venues, the physical spaces where you'll work. Your ideal teaching location might be a yoga studio, gym, health resort, or your living room. Maybe your dream job is working exclusively at yoga and music festivals, or perhaps you'd like to livestream classes from your garage. Most ideas are possible, so give yourself permission to dream.

Next, I'd like you to think about geography. Where in the world would you like to be based? Perhaps you live in Northern

England, and you'd like to see the sunshine a little more often. Maybe you live in a small town, and you know if you moved to the city, you'd have access to a larger pool of potential students. It's your life and your business, so you get to decide where it will happen.

- What venues would be best for you? (studio, gym, home, online)
- What are the advantages of the city or town where you live now?
- What are the disadvantages?
- What would be the best place, geographically, for you to be based?
- How might things change in one, two, or three years?

There is a reason why actors tend to move to New York or Los Angeles, and it's no coincidence that high-tech entrepreneurs move to Silicon Valley. That's where the most opportunities are in their fields. As a yoga teacher, it's never quite as obvious, but if you analyze both your potential venues and geographical location carefully, you can often make choices more conducive to success.

Some teaching venues are competitive and underpaid, others are highly paid with almost no one applying for work. Some cities are expensive, with low teachers' salaries, while others are desperate for teachers and the pay is high. I'm fully aware that not everyone can pick up and move on a whim, but analyze your situation honestly and take into consideration all the factors that will help or hinder your success.

WHEN

As I sat around that campfire all those years ago, I gave myself a one-year timeline to go from idea to launch. I was teaching like crazy, and I knew I needed to make a big move within twelve months, or I was going to implode. With that in mind, my final question for you is *when* do you want and need to take action?

- Are you able to start right now?
- Financially, should you start part time, as a side gig?
- Are there any big life events (weddings, births, house moves) on the horizon?
- Do you have existing work contracts to fulfill?
- Do you have financial obligations that will affect your timing?

I like to tell teachers that "now is always the best time," but there are many reasons why that might not be the case. Sometimes, there are very real-life events and responsibilities that make it necessary to wait and plan for your big move. Sometimes, rather than wait, maybe the wisest decision is to start your new yoga business on nights and weekends. Even though I want you to jump headfirst into this new business venture, I don't want you to take unnecessary risks.

Money Expands Your Values

Money is simply a store of value, and the more money you have, the more you can explore what means the most to you, whether that is family, travel, free time, or contribution. Many yoga teachers find it hard to get excited about financial targets, but those same people are excited to do more of the things they love.

- What do you value most?
- If you had more money today, what would you do?
- What areas of your life would you love to expand?
- When you have a day to yourself, how do you use your time?

Some people value their home life, and as they earn more, they invest in making their house a place of comfort and joy. Others value travel, and as their earnings increase, they're able to explore more of the world. Some teachers simply want more free time, so if they earn more per hour, they can work less. What do you value? What's important for you?

YOUR FINANCES TODAY

For much of my life, I was so anti-money that I deliberately ignored tracking anything financial. I didn't know how much money I made each month, I didn't know my total expenses, and I ignored my bank balance completely. Luckily, I didn't spend beyond my means, but my "go with the flow" attitude still came with a huge cost.

For over a decade, I was anxious about money every single day. Would I be able to pay rent? What if I got sick and couldn't teach for a week? Could I save enough for the trip I'd planned over the holidays? Before you set financial goals, let's first get honest about your immediate needs.

- What is your average monthly income?
- How much is your rent or mortgage payment?

- How much are your monthly transportation costs?
- How much do you spend on healthcare monthly?
- What is your average expenditure on food and entertainment?

Financial security comes when your monthly expenses are easily covered by your income and you have enough left over to cover surprise costs that will inevitably arise. I'd encourage you to use Google Sheets or Excel to list all your sources of monthly income and all your monthly expenses. You don't need to hire an accountant or download a special app (unless you want to). Simply map out your income and spending for the past two months in a spreadsheet, and then update it moving forward.

With your income and expenses clear, now you know how much your new yoga business should earn to at least match your current financial needs. If your new business is an expansion of your current teaching work, everything you earn will be a net gain, so that's easy. If this new venture is meant to replace another non-yoga income source, you'll want to plan carefully so as not to put too much pressure on yourself during the early days.

WHAT ARE YOU WILLING TO GIVE UP?

To build a business, you'll need to give up something you're spending time on now. This is how a value exchange works. Over the years, I've given up more things than I can count as I grew my business. Some sacrifices were worth it, others were not.

When my middle son was young, I was almost always working in the afternoons and didn't pick him up from day care or spend time with him in the park in the afternoons. That was a mistake.

I can't get those moments back, and it wasn't worth the business growth I achieved.

During that same period, I quit drinking and gave up dozens of nights out with friends. It was hard to let those friendships go, but that trade was worth it for sure. Those people and those outings were not aligned with my mission, and I made the right decision to put my energy elsewhere.

- What leisure activities or hobbies would you be willing to cut to make time for your new business venture?
- If you needed to work six or even seven days a week at first, would that be worth it for you at this stage of your life?
- Yoga teachers often need to work nights and weekends when students can more easily join their classes—would that be something you'd consider?
- Are there some non-negotiables for you in terms of work, schedule, and commitments?
- What about time with your friends, intimate partner, and family?

You'll have to give up something to grow your business, so take time to think this through carefully. If you overextend yourself like I did, your career might end up cutting you off from the activities and people you value most. On the other hand, if you're not willing to give up anything, you won't get very far.

TARGET MONTHLY INCOME

Now it's time to choose your target monthly income. This should be a figure that feels ambitious yet realistically achievable within the next six months. Your financial target should be enough to cover your current expenses, and it should also factor in an increase to justify the extra effort you're making.

Most teachers worry about underearning, but the even greater risk is to overshoot and overcommit like I did. If you take on too much, too soon, the personal sacrifices required can make any financial gain seem frivolous. Many yoga teachers get so caught up in their blossoming teaching career, for example, that they miss the opportunity to start a family. For some, this is deliberate, and they have no regrets. For many more, it's a terrible loss, and the ends never justify the means.

Early on, what I *really* wanted was simple. I wanted to have health insurance, to support a family, to travel, and to feel like I could pick and choose teaching gigs based on what I was passionate about, not just because of a paycheck. I could have accomplished all of this (and much more) without giving up my entire personal life for two years after opening that first studio. I want you to aim high, but aim carefully so that when you get what you want, you'll be happy on the other side.

Success on Your Own Terms

Sheila landed her dream job at a large yoga studio and taught there for eight years. Initially, her strongest value was travel, and every three months or so, she flew off on some new adventure. She did this for years, but at age thirty-eight, her biological clock started ticking, and building a family became her number one priority. She didn't have much time.

Sheila shifted half her teaching to private clients, which increased her income by nearly 40 percent over a two-month period.

She also insisted her clients come to her apartment as she deliberately constructed a work-life setup that was conducive to motherhood. A year later, when she met her husband and got pregnant, she quickly shifted her entire teaching schedule to privates and was able to teach right up until month eight.

Six weeks after giving birth to her son, she returned to teaching her private clients again from home, and in the years that followed, she took a very deliberate and crafted approach to her teaching and her time. Most teachers could do what Sheila did, but most never will. It took planning, clarity, and vision. Sheila created success on her own terms. My hope is that you'll do the same.

CHAPTER VI

Where to Teach
(In-Person)

R afael was my first real yoga teacher. He was strict, bone thin, and wore nothing but tiny shorts. Every night, thirty-one of us packed into a disgusting carpeted studio on Spring Street, sweating together for ninety minutes. Soon enough, I was super skinny like my teacher, rigid in my approach to yoga, and I too wore tiny spandex (oops). Until I arrived in Bangkok, that formative experience became my primary reference for what a yoga studio and yoga teaching looked like.

In Bangkok, I heard about a Thai teacher hosting daily classes in Lumpini Park, right in the middle of the city. Out of curiosity, I showed up to class one morning; to my surprise, I joined eight other students who had all paid to slip around on bamboo mats for an hour. It was a little hard to concentrate, but the class worked, and this teacher was making a living with zero overhead costs. I didn't know something like this was possible.

Today, everyone knows about yoga in the park, but did you know about yoga in schools, nursing homes, doctors' offices, hotels, and human resources departments? In 2016, Yoga Alliance, in conjunction with *Yoga Journal*, released an extensive research project called *Yoga in America*. One of the most interesting findings was that more people were practicing yoga outside the studio than inside—a trend that has only increased in the years since.

As a teacher, this is great news. It means you're no longer beholden to the four walls of a yoga center or to the limited opportunities offered by studio owners and managers. You can now earn more, teach what you want, and take full control over your schedule and career.

In this chapter, we'll explore some of the top in-person teaching opportunities right now. This list will inevitably be incomplete, as opportunities continue to sprout up daily, but hopefully, it will help break through your limiting beliefs about how and where yoga can be taught.

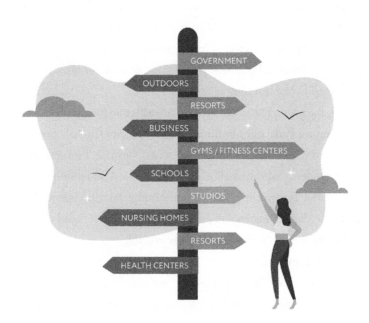

STUDIOS

Rather than thinking of yoga studio gigs as your destination, think about them as an exciting step along your journey. As I've mentioned, there are more opportunities outside of studios than inside, but studio work remains an important part of a yoga teaching portfolio. These days, my graduates and I spend more time teaching in alternative venues, but teaching in a purpose-built venue is always fun and feels like coming home.

Pros of Yoga Studio Teaching Gigs:
- Positive environment
- Purpose-built for yoga, often with props, mirrors, etc.
- Receptive clients
- Ease of marketing

Cons:
- Limited number of classes available
- Limited capacity in each class
- Most studios have a small membership base
- One studio owner/manager usually has control
- Pay and earning potential are limited

GYMS AND FITNESS CENTERS

Many yoga teachers used to look down on gym yoga, since it was often taught by unqualified teachers and the quality was low. This is no longer true. Some of the best-paid, best-attended classes are now in gyms, and the facilities can be amazing. Gyms are often larger and better equipped, and their membership base can be ten times larger than that of a yoga studio, so it's easier to fill a class or workshop.

When considering a gym, the biggest concerns are the practice room, attendance patterns, and class etiquette. At some gyms, students are allowed to come in and out as they please, talk on phones, and even do other exercises while in your sessions. This is a nonstarter for many teachers, so do check in advance. You should also be aware that although there are very-high-paid gym gigs, the average gym pays less than most yoga studios.

Pros of Gym Gigs:
- Lots of gyms, lots of opportunities
- Large timetable of classes
- Large membership base
- Extensive facilities
- Opportunities for workshops and intensives
- Ease of marketing

Cons:
- Average pay tends to be low
- Noise and distraction can be an issue
- Gym clients are not always the best yoga clients
- High member churn means new people every time

BOUTIQUE FITNESS CENTERS

Boutique fitness centers include pole fitness studios, rock climbing gyms, CrossFit boxes, gymnastics centers, and dance studios. Although these fitness centers tend to focus on their own discipline, many also

offer their clients yoga as an added value. They do this to keep their clients engaged and to monetize the downtime in their facilities.

For example, CrossFit boxes often have a mobility class on the schedule a couple of times a week, and many rock climbing gyms offer regular yoga sessions. Every center is unique, but these are great places to find affinity groups of highly motivated students and business partners.

Pros of Boutique Fitness Centers:
- Very little competition for jobs
- Motivated and highly interested students
- New and unique work experience for you
- Higher pay than most venues

Cons:
- Limited schedule availability for extra activities like yoga
- Facilities can be challenging, with visual obstructions or exercise equipment in the middle of the space
- Unpredictable class attendance and sign-ups

OUTDOOR CLASSES

Outdoor classes are very popular and cost-effective to run, but the weather and local laws will dictate whether this opportunity is right for you. Legally, there are different rules in different cities, and most teachers who operate outdoors are in a legal gray zone. This means they do not technically have permits or permission, but no one has asked them to stop.

Teachers often conduct classes in parks, on beaches, and on paved courts in recreational areas. I have also seen outdoor classes on school and university campuses, in parking lots, and in picnic areas. Although soft surfaces like grass and sand look welcoming, hard, flat surfaces are always an easier and cleaner option for serious practice. I have conducted gray-zone classes at beaches and picnic areas, attended by more than one hundred people. I've conducted full permit classes on hotel lawns and in convention center lots. Outdoor classes are always a fun experience and students love them. If you're considering this option, the biggest challenge is projecting your voice, particularly if you're competing with the sound of the ocean or wind.

Pros of Outdoor Classes:
- Zero overhead costs
- Location itself can be a selling point
- Lots of options to choose from
- Fun and challenging teaching experience

Cons:
- Weather can be unpredictable or even impossible
- Local laws and rules may limit opportunities
- Noise, dirt, bugs, and uneven surfaces cause problems
- It's difficult to project your voice
- Unwanted spectators can be awkward (or creepy)

SCHOOLS

It's exciting to see yoga increasingly offered in schools, particularly private schools. The big roadblock to full adoption, however, is that many yoga teachers insist on integrating religion and spirituality into their classes. If you're interested in teaching in schools, it's important to present your classes like an elective activity or after-school sport. Ensure your proposed program is 100 percent secular or you'll run into problems getting anything approved.

Getting these gigs can be slow and complicated, and pre-screening might include drug testing, background checks, insurance requirements, and reference checks.

Any classes targeting ages twelve or younger should be considered kids' yoga. Kids' classes must be short, playful, and fast paced to hold their attention. This usually means a thirty-minute session with animal poses, games, guided breathing, and a minute or two of silence. Teen yoga, often called young adult yoga, is indistinguishable from adult classes in terms of structure, but forty-five-minute sessions are preferable to deal with the shorter attention spans of students.

Pros of After-School Yoga:
- Daytime hours (no late nights or weekends)
- High-pay, long-term commitment
- Reliable student base, term-long connection
- Predictable schedule
- High-value, meaningful work
- Very low competition
- Possibility to create a new program from scratch

Cons:
- Limited opportunities
- Four- to eight-month launch timeline is common
- Practice room is not always ideal
- Students are sometimes there involuntarily
- Complex hiring/contract process

NURSING HOMES/GOLDEN YEARS YOGA

The world is rapidly aging, and older people today are wealthier and healthier than at any time in history. Yoga is an amazing tool to help the elderly live their best lives, and yet almost no one is offering what I like to call Golden Years Yoga. At the time of this writing, I know only two teachers actively pursuing this, and they are doing very well financially. From what they've shared with me, the work has been extremely rewarding too.

If you're interested in teaching in this market, there are two big challenges you need to consider. First, you'll need training and expertise in working with age-related mobility issues. Almost every client will have an injury, physical limitation, doctor's orders, or other medical issue that you'll need to consider. As with schools, you'll likely need to maneuver through a fair amount of paperwork and bureaucracy, but if you're excited to work with seniors, don't get scared off. Dive in and start learning.

Pros of Golden Years Yoga:
- Great pay
- Daytime hours (no nights or weekends)
- Motivated and committed students
- Important, meaningful work
- Excellent facilities

Cons:
- Difficult jobs to land
- Insurance and liability issues can be onerous
- Additional training and experience might be required
- Very challenging classes to teach
- Complex hiring/contract process

CORPORATE YOGA

Collectively, companies like Facebook, Google, General Electric, and Unilever spend tens of millions of dollars annually on office gyms, speakers, trainers, nutritionists, dietitians, and yoga teachers. From the company's perspective, when they invest in their employees' health, they see an immediate return on their investment if staff become happier, are more at peace, and get sick less often.

Some companies make wellness spending decisions unilaterally, but more often, decisions are made independently in each department, by individual executives or directors. To land these gigs, you need to find the person or people in charge of the budget for one specific department. Unless you or someone you know is on the inside, finding that decision maker is usually the most challenging task.

Corporate gigs tend to be high paid, during daytime hours, and very exciting to teach. If things go well, they very often turn into long-term contracts. Finding these jobs can require some serious hustle, but they can be lucrative and rewarding long term.

Pros of Corporate Yoga:
- Great pay
- Very little competition
- Daytime hours (no nights or weekends)
- Long-term contracts
- Motivated and willing students

Cons:
- Very slow hiring process
- Lots of bureaucracy

- Approvals can linger indefinitely
- Decision maker can be hard to find
- Payment is usually net thirty or even sixty days

HEALTH CENTERS AND RESORTS

Wellness centers, spas, and health resorts commonly offer group and private classes to their clients. An offering might be a one-on-one session in a consultation room in an urban health center, or it might be a group class under a pagoda at a destination health resort. For example, I used to teach an 8:00 a.m. class on the beach at a health resort on Koh Samui Island, and I later taught private classes in a tiny room at an urban spa. I earned about twenty dollars per class on the beach and nearly eighty dollars per class in the city. This is typical.

Today, destination health resorts often have a teacher in residence who leads one to two classes daily. The pay at these resort gigs tends to be low, but the experience can be well worth it, since the teaching environment is ideal and the clients are often yoga fanatics already.

Pros of Spas and Health Resorts:
- Great environment for teaching
- Great clients and employers
- Pay is high in urban areas
- Very little competition in urban areas
- Interesting and changing clientele

Cons:
- Pay is low in resort areas
- Competition is high in resort areas
- Client churn is high

MEETUP.COM

Meetup.com is one of the very first social networking sites for local events, and it's still going strong today. The site is based around people meeting in social groups, usually in person, and serves everyone from chess fanatics to marathon runners. The sports and fitness groups are among the most active; many have dozens or even hundreds of members who meet locally each week.

On any given day, in most areas around the world, Meetup groups engage in various activities, including yoga. For yoga teachers, this presents the obvious opportunity to found a group yourself, build it up over time, and create a following. This is a great idea you should consider.

The second approach is to piggyback on existing groups so you can gain traction sooner. This is done by contacting the organizers of other fitness groups and offering a free fifteen-minute stretching session after their next meeting. Let's imagine it's a Saturday running group. They all run ten kilometers together, and you meet them afterwards for a fifteen-minute stretching routine in the park.

If you're serious about this opportunity, it's smart to combine both approaches simultaneously. Building your own group will give you the opportunity to charge money and develop a community based around you and your style of yoga over time. Making cameo appearances in other groups will allow you to gain interest for your group and will inevitably lead to other paid private or group classes as more people learn of your services.

Pros of Meetup.com:
- Low or no cost to get started
- Millions of active fitness users
- Lots of opportunities, very little competition

- Easy and fun networking
- Opportunity for you to be a leader

Cons:

- Many groups are non-commercial (free)
- New groups take time to launch and grow

AIRBNB EXPERIENCES

Airbnb Experiences are local classes, tours, and events offered in addition to Airbnb's typical room and home rentals. In the same way Airbnb doesn't own the properties on their platform, they also don't provide the experiences. People like you can offer experiences, and Airbnb simply takes a 20-percent commission.

For yoga teachers, this can be an exciting way to tap into Airbnb's huge database of clients, accept online payment, gain reviews, and earn money. Please don't be intimidated by partnering with a big company like Airbnb. They actively seek out and promote local teachers like you because they feel it's more in line with their brand than working with yoga studios or gyms.

The classes you offer here need to be an experience, meaning not just a private yoga class but also something more. Yoga on the beach at sunset, for example, or a yoga brunch. Maybe you offer a half-day mind-body experience that includes a nature hike, a yoga class, and a guided meditation session. On the low end, Airbnb Experiences start around twenty dollars on average, and the higher-end events are over one hundred dollars per person, so you have lots of options.

To learn more about this opportunity, start by searching experiences in your area to see what others are offering. If you see events with dozens or even hundreds of reviews, that's a good sign! It means people are actively and regularly signing up, so there's probably space for you too.

Pros of Airbnb Experiences:
- Free to join
- Huge exposure to potential clients
- Very little competition
- High earning potential
- Low 20-percent commission to Airbnb
- Unique way to combine yoga with other activities

Cons:
- Experiences are usually one-off since clients are travelers
- Experiences are usually more complex than a typical class
- Your area might not have many tourists

ONLINE BULLETIN BOARDS

Imagine a corkboard outside a grocery store where people pull numbers off printed flyers. This is how online bulletin boards function. Bulletin boards may feel outdated, but they attract heavy traffic, making them great places to find clients for private yoga, outdoor yoga, or other classes you're hosting independently. Studio posts are discouraged (or prohibited), so use bulletin board sites to promote your independent classes.

Bulletin board sites vary from country to country, but popular sites include Thumbtack.com, Craigslist.com, and Gumtree.co.uk.

Pros:

- Low or no cost to post
- Millions of users you can potentially reach
- Simple and easy to get started

Cons:

- Can be hard to promote group classes and other events
- Limited audience reach

Choose Your Own Adventure

One benefit of teaching yoga is that you can choose your own adventure. No doubt you will immediately think of obvious options such as studio classes, but if you broaden your horizons, you'll realize how many different—and potentially more fulfilling—paths are open to you.

A friend of mine, Natalie, landed a job teaching abroad at the Mandarin Oriental Hotel in northern Thailand. As part of her employment package, she received a stable monthly salary, accommodation, and food. Her workday was short, and she got to spend an entire year in a place most people only are able to visit for a few days, once in their lives.

Another colleague, Nina, worked on yachts for many years. Sometimes she worked on cruise ships, but the majority of her business came in the form of teaching on private yachts sailing in the Mediterranean. She earned around $1,000 a day to teach a one-hour class to owners and another for the crew. Her accommodation was paid for, as was food. At the end of a week, she would often walk off the ship with $5,000.

One last story. Before he became a yoga teacher, Edwin used to work as an administrative coordinator at city hall. The city council had a health budget that it hadn't used. After getting certified to teach, Edwin went back to his old colleagues and offered to be the resident yoga teacher for the city's employees. The job came with the salary, benefits, and pension plan typical of a public sector job. He taught two to three classes per day at various government offices, and it was an amazing success story for him both personally and professionally.

It's a great time to be a yoga teacher. Opportunities are all around you right now,

inside and outside of yoga studios. My challenge to you is to open your mind, knock on doors, and start exploring your options.

CHAPTER VII

How to Teach Online

M y studio group included three locations, sixteen teachers, and thousands of members. We were arguably the top yoga destination in Barcelona, and one of the best in all of Spain. It had taken my life savings and years of struggle to finally reach profitability, and I was beginning to see a light at the end of the tunnel.

And then came COVID-19. In March 2020, the government forced us to close down.

On a Zoom call, I told my staff I didn't think we'd ever be able to open again. Most of my team thought I was catastrophizing. This would all be over in a matter of weeks, they said. But I'd been following the virus closely. I remembered SARS well, and I was certain this was a life-changing event that would reshape the yoga industry forever.

Local businesses operate on the razor's edge, financially speaking. It's not uncommon for restaurants, bars, or yoga studios to have just enough cash reserves to cover two to four weeks of operational costs. Any lockdown, no matter how short, quickly turns into a financial disaster. When COVID-19 hit, I needed to make some hard decisions quickly because every day I delayed meant thousands more lost euros.

Since everyone was working from home, I went into the office. All alone, I ran through every possible scenario a dozen times. What if there were a vaccine? What if we were given grants or loans? What if social security grants provided extended help? Could we wait it out? Even my most optimistic projections left me flat broke before summer. I had commercial leases on properties I could not use, salaries to pay to staff who were not allowed to work, and there was no end in sight.

During those early days of the pandemic, everyone in Barcelona went outside at 8:00 p.m. to bang on pots and pans in an act of solidarity. With so little agency over our lives, this nightly ritual was a very tribal way for people to support healthcare workers and each other. The second Wednesday after lockdown, as my neighbors started banging their pans, I stepped out onto my terrace, and I broke down. I knew what I had to do.

The government offered low-interest loans to help local businesses, so I maxed out on this proposition and borrowed €50,000. First, I refunded all my students with active memberships. Next, I gave my staff severance packages. Finally, I settled all outstanding bills with our vendors. Some of the teachers were understanding, but many were angry, even vengeful. They felt I was using this pandemic as an excuse for a mass firing. This loss of my team's trust hurt much more than losing my life savings.

In the span of a few days, I went from a buzzing office and a huge team all around me to working all alone day and night to try to salvage what remained of my company. In a hurry, I did what everyone did during that period. I went online. I learned how to set up Zoom, how to use my camera and laptop to film, and then I immediately dived headfirst into live classes.

I remember twenty-three people logged in for my first pandemic class, and by the following Monday, we had over sixty students joining me from living rooms around the world. Not bad! Soon, I started maxing out at one hundred students and had to upgrade my Zoom account. By the end of that first year, I'd taught a record class with 13,467 people registered.

In my old yoga teaching life, my biggest-ever class was attended by sixty-three students—and that was just one time. Teaching online, even my small classes attracted more than a hundred attendees. My mind was blown. I didn't even know this was possible.

I was no stranger to online yoga. I'd been streaming free classes and social media content for more than a decade, but for the first time in my teaching career, all my students had fast internet connections. Even more importantly, the technology finally worked.

It was a perfect storm, destructive and creative all at once. The pandemic pushed online yoga forward by five to ten years overnight. It was nothing short of a revolution, and that momentum has only increased since March 2020. One door closed, and five more opened.

Online, there were no waiting lists or class size limits, and I rapidly broke through every imaginable glass ceiling. I was excited to discover that virtual classes expanded the market and allowed me to serve students in rural and geographically isolated areas, students who had never previously had access to yoga of any type.

In this chapter, I'll share what I've learned from teaching thousands of online classes, workshops, and training events.

The Good, the Bad, the Challenging

To date, I have taught as many classes online as I have in person. Some days, I log as many as six virtual teaching hours, and in a typical year, I'll now connect with over one hundred thousand students live. Amazing!

This doesn't mean you should focus exclusively on teaching online. If you're like most teachers I know, you probably don't want to give up in-person teaching altogether. Business-savvy teachers rightly say yes to both virtual and in-person opportunities because the fluid integration of the digital and real world has become the norm in all areas of life. Every teaching gig has its benefits and drawbacks of course, so let's look at the good, the bad, and the challenges of this new and growing opportunity.

The Good:
- Convenient (for you and students)
- Ultra-niche classes are possible
- Truly scalable
- You can teach students living anywhere
- You can record, review, and share classes afterwards
- Low or no overhead costs to operate

The Bad:
- Less personal
- Live attendance rates can be low
- Difficult to create a vibe
- Online students are often in a rush
- Tech glitches do happen

The Challenges:
- Classes must be engaging, or students will leave
- Online teaching requires different teaching skills
- More moving parts, more complexity

Local Heroes, Online Leaders

When yoga moved online, my biggest fear was that celebrity teachers would steal all my students. With the option to practice with any teacher in the world, why would students choose me? I'm a skilled instructor with a loyal following, but I'm certainly not a media personality.

Fortunately, my fears were unjustified. As the yoga world migrated online, both my classes and those of my graduates grew and grew and grew. I learned that many celebrity teachers were famous for being famous, not for their teaching. They looked great in photos and interviews, but they couldn't deliver effective classes the way our teachers could. Online, meritocracy rules, and the yoga market has splintered into thousands of niche communities where you can become a local hero and online leader.

Live Classes, Fresh Content

Why do you watch today's new report today but never tomorrow? Why are the sports scores from today's games interesting while last week's scores are irrelevant? For whatever reason, we humans seem hardwired for real-time activities, and this is why, in most cases, live online classes will outsell video on-demand offerings by two to ten times. The internet is full of on-demand videos, yet ironically much of this content drives an ever-increasing demand for live events.

It gets even weirder. Besides live classes, the next best thing is a freshly recorded class. Why would a class that was filmed earlier today or last night be more interesting than a recorded class from last week or last year? I don't know the answer, but I have years of data telling me this is true.

Here's how this plays out in a real-world scenario. You know your students crave live classes, so that's where you focus most of your efforts. Your live classes themselves might have an 80-percent, 50-percent, or even meager 20-percent show-up rate, but don't be discouraged. The majority of those who miss your live class will be completely satisfied as long as they receive access to the recording as soon as possible. Most students practice along with the recording in the first day or two after its release, and then you'll see your replay views drop to almost nothing a week later. Students love live classes and fresh content. Very few teachers understand this, and if you do, you'll find it easier and more profitable to operate your business.

Focus on Teaching, Not on Tech

We're living in the golden age of yoga media production, and oddly, nobody really cares. Open any social media app, and you'll be bombarded with Hollywood-caliber content all day long: full wheel pose on the side of a cliff at sunset, handstand press demonstrations shot by drones, and even 360-degree camera angles to reveal every detail of a pose. Oddly, most of that content is ignored. You and I might notice it because we're in the business, but our students scroll right past it.

Students today care about the same things as always: stress, back pain, aging, their monkey minds, loneliness, loss of mobility, sleep problems, and anxiety. No one is worried about 4K video, stop motion sun salutes, or your post-production color correction.

If you want to excel in online yoga, focus on teaching, not on the technical aspects of media production. There is no special camera, drone, or video editor that will make or break your classes.

The way to teach great classes online is to leverage the hardware tools you most likely already own and put most of your time and attention into your class experience itself. Let's take a look.

Standard Tech Setup:
- Phone as your webcam
- Tripod for your phone
- Laptop as "command center" for classes
- Bluetooth earbuds
- Light source

I own all kinds of video and lighting equipment, but I never use any of it for my live classes. The setup I'll share with you is the same one my team and I use every day. I actually carry my entire kit in my backpack with me at all times. I like to teach yoga; I'm not a filmmaker. You're probably the same. So remember, simple is best; less is more.

YOUR PHONE

If your phone is less than three years old, it's your best choice for a live streaming camera. It'll outperform even the most expensive external webcams you might see advertised online. Since you know how to use your phone better than any other device you own, it's the best piece of hardware for you to use for your classes. If your phone is old, if the battery doesn't hold a charge anymore, or if it's running out of internal storage, you might consider an upgrade. Whenever you do buy a new phone, as a yoga teacher, it's always worth buying the newest and best phone you can afford, with as much storage as possible. It'll make your teaching life easier.

PHONE TRIPOD

My team and I use cheap tripods (around $20) that are specifically designed for phones. We like the cheap ones because they're light, they're versatile, and we can easily afford to keep one in every room that we use for teaching. I always keep an extra one in my backpack too, just in case. I'm embarrassed to admit that I also own a fancy $300 tripod, but I never use it. It's huge, heavy, and a big hassle.

If you don't have a tripod, don't let that stop you. I've taught many classes with my phone attached to a broomstick with a rubber band. You can also prop your phone up with pillows, on a bookcase, or on your desk. Provided you find a good filming angle, your students won't even know the difference.

LAPTOP

Think of your laptop as your command center for your classes. This is where you'll control the sound, record the class, and moderate the chat room. Your phone is very powerful, but managing a class from that tiny screen is too tedious. If your laptop is less than five years old, it's almost certainly adequate for your needs.

BLUETOOTH EARBUDS

For live classes, sound quality is much more important than video quality. If students can hear you clearly, you can get away with poorly lit, low-resolution classes. But if they can't hear you, you'll get complaints in real time. There are two reasons I recommend earbuds. First, the mic stays the same distance from your mouth, so your volume is consistent throughout class and in various poses. Second, the battery life of modern earbuds tends to be excellent.

> **TIP:** My earbuds fall out when I do downward-facing dog, so I use inexpensive rubber ear hook accessories to keep them in place. You can order them online.

LIGHT SOURCE

Natural light is always the best, and I'd encourage you to use it whenever possible. When insufficient, turn on the overhead lights in your room and consider a cheap ring light you can purchase online for twenty to thirty dollars. They often come with their own tripod and a USB power cable. You could spend enormous amounts of time and money on complex lighting, but your students will appreciate it more if you spend that time planning for great classes.

The most common lighting mistake is to have your light source—whether that's a window or a ring light—behind you instead of in front of you. This creates a silhouette effect, and you'll be teaching in the shadows. A small backlight can be helpful, but always remember to look right into your primary light source. If light comes in from a window, for example, you should position your phone between you and the window and look at the light source as you teach.

SOFTWARE FOR LIVE CLASSES

My team and I have taught yoga on just about every livestream video platform available, and nothing beats Zoom. Zoom is an incredibly stable and robust piece of software that is consistently improving. On a typical day, my team and I spend anywhere between four and six hours in live Zoom sessions, all of which are recorded and exported. We've battle-tested Zoom every way possible, and I can tell you with confidence that it should be your default choice for online classes.

Many teachers get away with using the free version, but since that limits your class-time length and recording options, I recommend you upgrade to the lowest-level paid account.

What about live video on social media? I've taught many live events on YouTube, Facebook, Instagram, and TikTok. In some cases, I even set up private accounts or private groups, which I charged students to access. It was a good experiment, but today, I don't use any social media platforms for paid events. Social media is great for building and nurturing your community, but it's not a great place to host paid classes.

INTERNET SPEED AND WI-FI

A cabled internet connection provides the fastest speeds, but I don't like to add any more complexity to my setup. I teach exclusively on Wi-Fi. Both my laptop and my phone are connected to Wi-Fi, and I always ensure I'm getting a minimum of 20 Mbps (megabytes per second) of download speed and 10 Mbps of upload speed. In your home or office, the Wi-Fi is probably ten to fifty times that speed, but in certain locations, your signal might be weak. So always test beforehand.

In a pinch, it is possible to teach using your cell phone data as a hotspot. I've done this while on holiday in an Airbnb and even once in a field in Germany. Again, be sure to do a speed test before you start. In some cases, you might consider a test class with a friend to ensure you've got a strong enough signal.

YOUR SETUP FOR FILMING

None of your students will wake up today and think about your filming setup or room size. They'll think about the class itself and your teaching and how it can help them with their challenges. I've taught in hotel rooms as small as 150 square feet, I've taught big online classes in the park, and I've taught alone in dance studios large enough to hold one hundred students. The location doesn't matter; the class is what is important.

With any location, make sure to test in advance for light, sound, tripod, internet, and power. It's really helpful to work from the same location since you'll get comfortable with the setup. Below, you'll find some tips that I've found helpful in my own classes.

Helpful Tips:
- Teach indoors rather than outdoors to control light and noise.
- Close doors and windows, and turn off anything that makes sounds.
- Film in the same location so there are fewer variables.
- Plug in your laptop and phone so you don't need to worry about battery life.
- Ensure your earbuds are charged before class.
- Test your internet speed.

CAMERA POSITIONS

Teaching online is different from teaching in person, particularly with regard to your body language and body position. With the camera, it's helpful to distinguish between three primary positions: one meter away (camera 1), two meters away (camera 2), and three meters away (camera 3).

In camera 1 position, you'll stand approximately an arm's-length distance away from the screen, enabling your students to see you from the shoulders up. This is how you should begin and end your classes, and it's also a position you'll want to utilize strategically throughout each class to personalize the experience. Camera 1 position is not great for demonstrations, but it's extremely helpful for connecting on a personal level since students can see your eyes and micro-expressions.

Camera 2 position is approximately one big step back from the camera. Here, your students will see you from the waist up or possibly from the knees up. Students can still see some of your micro-expressions, but they can also see your hands, arm positions, neck, and shoulder demonstrations.

In camera 3 position, your whole body is visible. You can stand up with your arms above your head and everything from your fingertips to your toes will be visible. Camera 3 is where you'll teach much of your class, but don't get stuck there. Students can't see your face or your eyes well. This makes it difficult to relate to you as a person, increasing the likelihood that they will zone out and lose interest.

Skilled teachers alternate between all three positions throughout class, sometimes performing effective demonstrations at times and sometimes stepping in close to reconnect. Just as you move around the room when teaching in person, you need to move in and out from the camera when teaching online to make your class intimate, dynamic, and engaging.

Your default position will be eyes to camera in a portrait position. At times, you'll also want to utilize profile position, where you turn to the side at ninety degrees to demonstrate certain movements. Last and least frequently, there are times when you'll turn your back to the camera, in what I call reverse portrait stance, to demonstrate reverse prayer hands, shoulder blade retraction, or anything else that can be seen best from behind. Use reverse portrait sparingly, and don't turn your back for long or you'll lose your students' attention.

BODY LANGUAGE AND GESTURES

When you're teaching online, your body language needs to convey steadiness and confidence. Ground your feet, square your shoulders, and speak with authority. Avoid standing at strange angles, cropping half your head, or coming in so close you create a fish-eye effect. Awkward body language on camera will translate as a lack of competence to your students.

On camera, gestures need to be bigger. Your students might join your classes on their phones, in which case they'll see you on a tiny screen, often positioned at the edge of their mat. This means that your body language and gestures all need to be overplayed—almost theatrical—so that students can understand what's going on.

If you've ever watched a Shakespeare in the Park production, think about the way those actors move in an exaggerated manner compared to a screen actor. That's because the audience is far away. Because your student's screen is small and they aren't next to it, you need to emulate those over-gesturing theater actors.

CHANGING ANGLES

Teachers who work online quickly learn that one camera angle doesn't cut it for an entire class. If you move from a standing sequence to a floor sequence, for example, you'll need to tilt the camera downward. If you want to end your class in a seated position, you may move your tripod closer or drop it down to waist height in order to get a good camera 1 position as you finish.

Sometimes teachers worry that it's unprofessional to move the camera in real time, but if you do it quickly and efficiently, it makes your class experience more personable, relatable, and effective. No one is bothered by the five to ten seconds it takes for you to change your camera angle if it improves the class.

Tips from the Field

After teaching thousands of classes, I've learned dozens of tips and tricks. Here is my shortlist of the most important.

- **Camera on.** Encourage students to turn their cameras on. Sometimes, they will need a few classes to get comfortable with it, but it improves the experience for everyone.

- **Say their names.** Use your students' names throughout class. When you're teaching on Zoom, their names are right there for you on the screen, so say them. This type of personalized instruction makes a world of difference.

- **Download your attendance report.** As your classes get bigger, it can be difficult to remember who showed up to class and who didn't. Zoom has an attendance report that you should download to keep track of your community.

- **Upload recordings to YouTube.** YouTube allows you to make your videos public, unlisted, or private. Unlisted videos are fast, safe, and my preferred method since they do not require a password but are impossible to find without the link. Once your class is done, upload it to YouTube and share the unlisted link with your students.

- **Use the chat box like a yoga studio front desk.** Before class starts, chat with your students on camera or using the chat feature in Zoom. Ask questions, tell jokes, just be yourself. Remember, there are thousands of yoga videos online; people come to your class because they want to be around other people, so hang out.

Taking Chair Yoga Online

Prior to the pandemic, my colleague Stephanie taught chair yoga in elder care facilities. During the lockdowns, nursing homes were some of the first to close down, so Stephanie's classes were discontinued indefinitely. Instead of giving up, Stephanie taught herself Zoom and moved her programs online in a hurry.

Most of the facilities had televisions, or at least a projector where they could screen the classes, and someone on staff was able to handle the technology. Within a few months, Stephanie had restarted most of her previous classes online, and even more exciting, she started to expand to new facilities. Since teaching online removed the restrictions on her own travel, she lumped multiple groups together into the same class, and everyone was happier as a result.

Her senior clients were completely isolated from the world at that point, so to join a buzzing and growing group of peers every Tuesday and Thursday morning was a highlight of their week.

Teachers often think that as online classes grow in numbers, the quality diminishes, but that wasn't what happened in Stephanie's case. Her six original clients were delighted to be joined by the same number of attendees at two, three, and eventually six different facilities in different parts of her state. For those seniors, the onset of a pandemic was surely frightening and isolating, but thanks to Stephanie's classes, they met new friends, stayed active, and became part of a positive, supportive community through online yoga.

CHAPTER VIII

Time Management

When I taught group studio classes full time, I usually had one morning session and two evening classes, six days a week. I did my personal practice before the first class, so that left me with a huge block of six or even eight hours of free time in the middle of the day.

My long-term goal was to build my own yoga business, so the smart move would have been to use this abundant free time to plan and prepare for my anticipated future, but that's not what happened. Those midday breaks became a big blur of nothingness. I'd go for a walk, check my email, get lost down a rabbit hole of yoga websites, and then tinker around the house until it was time to head back to the studio to teach again.

Often, time management is even more challenging than the tasks you need to complete, and it's not as simple as setting up a calendar. To be productive, you need to plan when you'll do your new tasks, but you also need to ruthlessly cut other things from your life to make space for something new. Free time is important, but you also need to free up mental space for creative work.

In the years since my initial struggles, I've become hyperproductive. I can now accomplish more in one day than I previously accomplished in an entire week. I've read every time-management book I could find, hired coaches, and even attended live classes on productivity and organization. Everything helped, but ultimately, the approach that works best for me is simple, aggressive, and easy to learn.

In this chapter, I'll share with you my approach in hopes that it will help you develop your own system for getting things done.

Feed the Dragon

We've already discussed that the two real assets in a yoga business are *you* and *your community*. Think of these assets like a huge hungry dragon that must be fed every day. The food you'd feed an average pet simply won't do. After all, dragons blow fire; they're insatiable. As a business owner, you need to feed your dragon every day. What this looks like is one hour developing yourself and a second hour building and nurturing your community. You also need to practice yoga yourself, but it's possible to incorporate your practice into your other commitments.

If you practice yoga at home, for example, you can listen to audiobooks, personal-growth teachers, and even anatomy and physiology lectures while you do your yoga. Your daily practice itself can also be an investment in your *you* asset, particularly if you're practicing with a new teacher, learning a new style, or deepening your understanding of new techniques.

You Time Activities:
- Engaging in personal practice
- Reading or listening to relevant books
- Learning from relevant podcasts or YouTube videos
- Attending Meetup groups or masterminds with colleagues
- Engaging with colleagues in online groups and forums
- Seeking out professional training

- Working with coaches or experts to deepen your skills
- Attending professional courses and classes

Your Community Activities:
- Outreach emailing clients, employers, and partners
- Answering student questions via email, SMS, or social media
- Creating and sharing high-value educational content
- Attending events (online or off-line)
- Participating in relevant groups, message boards, and chat rooms

What happens if you don't feed the dragon? It gets hungry and starts to get thinner and smaller. Your students, employers, and potential business partners will quickly start looking elsewhere.

Get Rid of Time Vultures

Free time alone is not enough to get things done. You also need to free up your mental real estate so there's room to add in something new. Without realizing it, most of us have hundreds of useless ideas, shock-and-awe news stories, pop culture narratives, and endless chatter filling our brains to the brim. Until you get rid of these time vultures, focus and productivity will always be fleeting.

Let's start with social media. When I check the stats on many of my clients' phones, their usage report shows they spend an average of four to six hours a day on various apps: Instagram, Facebook, YouTube, TikTok. If they were teaching classes or talking to students on those apps, that would be one thing, but 90 percent of that time is mindless scrolling.

Here's how to get back your social media time. First, both iOS and Android have time-out settings where you can block the app from yourself. I set my time-out limit to fifteen minutes per app per day, and that's it. Next, drag all your social apps to the last screen on your phone—all the way to the right so they are harder to access. If you want to go one step further, you can even put all those apps into a folder on that last screen. Although this may seem silly, it's effective; when those apps are out of sight, you're less likely to open them in the first place.

Next, I want you to unfollow at least 10 percent of your contacts. If you want to be aggressive, aim for 30 percent. I'd also like to suggest you block at least three people too. Use this simple heuristic: if someone is not part of your life today and you cannot foresee them in your life in the future, unfollow them and let them live in your memories. If someone triggers a negative emotional response every time you see them, such as an ex or former boss, unfollow and block them. Within a day or two, these people will disappear from your consciousness, creating space for new people and new projects.

I started as a heavy social media user early on, but that changed for me when some random person contacted me on Facebook. Her name was Tracy, and apparently, she and I used to walk to school together when we were five years old. She'd found me on Facebook and wanted to say hi. So what did I do? I did what we all do: I went to her profile and spent the next half hour clicking through her family vacation pictures, wedding photos. I basically eavesdropped on her life. Let me be clear: I have zero recollection of this person, and although I'm sure she's a kind (nonpsychopathic) person, I'd given her thirty minutes of my Thursday. And why? Because she messaged me. That was time I could have used to build my business, to practice yoga, or to call my mother. At the very least, I could have done some errands around the house—anything!

I'm sure you've had similar experiences yourself, but that day, everything changed for me. My Facebook friend list was maxed out at five thousand people, and I unfriended them all. I also unfollowed just about everyone on all social media platforms, including true friends and family members. I realized that every single time I opened my phone, I needed to be on guard. Social media apps are designed to lure you into spending your whole day scrolling and clicking on ads, so your job, as a business owner and someone who respects the value of time, is to stop doing free work for Big Tech.

Next, let's talk about the news. Stop watching or listening in real time. Today's news is a rough draft of history, so give it some time to settle in. If you like to stay informed, read or listen to a daily recap. For example, I receive a short email summary of the most important world news stories of the week. It's a boring, image-free email. It's fact based and keeps me informed, but it doesn't spark powerful emotions. The collective news of the world is just too much for any of us to process in real time, so don't even try.

The next time vultures to get rid of are the people in your life who are black holes for energy. These are the friends who *only* call when they are in crisis, never when things are going well. They are the relatives who are always negative and defeated, never uplifting or supportive. They are the colleagues who embrace conspiracy theories, victim mentalities, and "the end is near" outlooks on life. This is hard, but these people have to go. I'm not suggesting you act cruelly or ghost people, but I am suggesting you respond more slowly to messages, change dinners into coffee meetups, and little by little, take back your time.

The final time vulture you need to address consists of events and social gatherings that suck your energy. If your friends host a monthly movie night that you've grown tired of, stop going. If your friends have drinking parties that go until 3:00 a.m. and that, while fun, you always regret, just stop. Most of us fill our lives with low-value activities; when you cut them, you'll make space in your head for new people, new ideas, and a creative new future.

Your Assignment:
- Unfollow at least 10 percent of your contacts.
- Block at least three people.
- Unsubscribe from as many email lists as possible.
- Hide your social media apps on the last screen of your phone.
- Add fifteen-minute timers to limit your social apps.
- Say no to at least one social invite this week.

Follow People of Influence, Not Influencers

Online influencers are usually celebrities or media personalities who are good at attracting attention. Ignore these people completely, and instead follow people you'd like to learn from. I call these *people of influence*, as opposed to influencers. Perhaps you know a teacher three years your senior you'd like to learn from. Follow her! Perhaps there is an anatomy teacher or wellness coach who publishes great information that can help you with your clients. Follow him too! Aim to find at least three, but a maximum of five, people of influence you can follow closely for the next month. As soon as you follow these people, I want you to message them right away. Here's what to say:

Hi, NAME, thanks for posting such great content. I'm a yoga teacher, and I've learned so much from your posts. Just wanted to let you know...

Very few people reach out to express genuine thanks, so you may be surprised how often you get a response. This is the first step toward building connections with people who might become the peers of your future, not ghosts of your past. This will inevitably open some new doors. In many cases, for both my graduates and myself, these simple outreach exercises have evolved into invitations to grab a coffee, the sharing of research, and even teaching collaborations.

They say you become the average of the four or five people you spend the most time with, but most of us don't have a peer group of other yoga business owners. The solution is to diligently curate your social media feed and create the next best thing: a virtual circle of people who influence and inspire you to be your best.

Each month, you might decide to unfollow some of your people of influence. Perhaps their messages are repetitive, or you simply feel you've learned enough. Great! Follow some new people of influence and repeat the process.

People of Influence to Consider:
- Yoga teachers with more experience/success
- Anatomy and biomechanics teachers

- Synergistic teachers: Pilates, physiotherapy, personal training
- Relevant teachers: health, wellness, nutrition
- Mind-body teachers: mindfulness, meditation, breathing
- Researchers in health, wellness, stress, exercise

People to Avoid Following:
- Business celebrities
- TV/movie celebrities
- Politicians
- Meme accounts
- Exes or crushes

Manage Your Phone and Computer

Years ago, I had lunch with a friend who owns a huge yoga business with sixty-five employees. As soon as we sat down, she put her phone in the middle of the table, so I followed her lead and did the same. My phone immediately lit up and vibrated; hers was black and silent. She looked at my phone, shrugged, and asked, "Really?" Embarrassed, I eventually turned my phone off completely and flipped it facedown. After our lunch, I sat on a bench outside the restaurant and immediately changed all my phone settings.

Now my phone delivers no push notifications whatsoever. No social media notifications, no messenger apps, no retail or delivery app notifications—nothing. My challenge to you is to turn everything off except notifications from family members who might need you in an emergency. Everyone else can wait. If your phone lights up every thirty seconds like mine did, you'll never get anything done. Your phone should be a silent, black screen, sitting there doing nothing until you need it to be of service to you.

Next, you need to think about your computer desktop and your physical desk or wherever you work. As I've mentioned, you need to create space for your new projects, and you can't do that if your workspaces are already filled with clutter. On your computer, ruthlessly file and delete things. If you're unsure or scared to act, just drag everything into a folder called "Miscellaneous." That'll do just fine for now. With your physical workspace, whether that is a desk or your kitchen table, get rid of the stacks of papers, empty the drawers of old bills, and create a blank canvas from which you can work.

Now that we've looked at your phone and your computer, I want to emphasize that your computer is where all your real work should happen, not your phone. Most of my clients are trying to run their entire business from the tiny screen of their phones. This is inefficient, and you cannot afford to waste time like this. Real work is done on a larger screen with a keyboard. No one operating at a high level is trying to do it all from a mobile device.

Your Assignment:
- Turn off all phone notifications.
- Silence your phone, always.
- Delete any phone app you haven't used in the past month.
- Clean up your computer desktop.
- Clean up your physical desk/workspace.
- Do real work with a keyboard and a screen, not your phone.

Change Your Passwords

Most people have one or two passwords they use for everything from online banking to their email service provider. For many of us, this password is silly or nostalgic, but I'd like you to make it aspirational instead. This way, every time you're prompted to log in to a website, you'll receive a reminder of your short- or long-term goals.

Examples of Aspirational Passwords:
- 10Kmonthlyrevenue!
- 12NewPrivateClients
- 6FigureYogaTeacher
- PrivateYogaPracticeSoldOut$!
- PublishedYogaAuthor!
- YogaForStressExpert#1!

Throw Stuff Away

Everything in your life carries some emotional weight. A cluttered attic contributes to your cluttered mind, even if indirectly. So in an effort to free up space, I'd like to challenge you to trash or donate at least 10 percent of everything in your house.

Get rid of old shoes, outfits you haven't worn in the past year, books you'll never read again, empty boxes, and kitchenware you don't use. This exercise can be just as uncomfortable as unfollowing people on social media, but for many, it's even more liberating. Make space.

Your Assignment:
- Trash or donate 10 percent (minimum) of your closet.
- Trash or donate 10 percent (minimum) of your kitchenware.
- Trash or donate 10 percent (minimum) of your books, papers, boxes, etc.

Buy Back Your Time

I had a mentor named Chris who was twelve years older than me and a successful real estate investor. He and I were out for a walk once, and a Rolls Royce drove by. Chris pointed to the man driving and said to me, "He's driving a Rolls Royce!" Apparently, this was the funniest thing Chris had ever seen. I didn't get it.

Chris explained that if you're wealthy enough to buy a $400,000 car, you shouldn't be driving it yourself. You should have a driver. Before he explained this, I never understood why Chris only used Uber and never drove, but suddenly I did. Time is way more valuable than money, and we're all running out of it. If you are fortunate enough to buy back some of your time, you should do it. And that doesn't necessarily mean having five-star services like drivers and personal assistants. It can start right away, today, with small tasks around the house.

The two simplest ways to buy back time involve food and cleaning. Based on my calculations, the average person spends eight to twelve hours per week on buying and preparing food and about five to seven hours on housekeeping chores. Some of this time is enjoyable: I love cooking, for example. And some of it is therapeutic: I find mopping the floor oddly calming. But all of that is time you cannot get back, so as soon as you're able to, you should buy back some of your time.

On a per-hour basis, entry-level yoga teachers earn at least three times as much as domestic house help. This means that if you teach one extra class per week, you could get three hours of house help. This quickly creates a surplus of time. If you're new to hiring house help, I know it can feel indulgent and even entitled. I grew up mowing lawns, washing cars, and doing odd jobs for money, so initially it was very difficult for me to hire help. But you must get over your own hang-ups.

As a yoga business owner, you need to create opportunities for others, not just yourself, and there are thousands of people looking for entry-level domestic jobs right now. Start by hiring someone to clean your bathroom, clean your kitchen, and do your laundry, for three hours on a Sunday. As you grow your business, you might get help with grocery shopping, food prep, and more. Once you see how much time you can free up, you'll start to understand how business works and you'll lay the groundwork for the inevitable future when you'll have a team of people supporting your business.

Use an Online Calendar

As yoga teachers, our calendars are crazy. You might have an 8:00 a.m. class on Monday and then the same day at 7:00 p.m., a live video conference. You cannot keep track of this in your head, and old-school paper calendars are not particularly useful either. Commit to the online calendar of your choice—Google Calendar or iCalendar are popular—and incorporate it into your work life. Make sure classes, calls, and even days for filming social media content are all scheduled.

There are lots of online booking tools, such as Calendly, that sync up with your digital calendar too. So as you grow your business, this will allow you to coordinate with clients and business partners more professionally. When I first started out as a yoga teacher, I carried my printed schedule in my backpack and checked it neurotically three times a day. Nothing has changed now except it's all digital. It's always updated on every device in real time, so I'm less neurotic and much more organized.

Calendar Tools to Consider:
- Google Calendar (free)
- iCalendar (free for iOS users)
- Calendly (free version available)

Give Yourself Deadlines

Without deadlines, no one would ever graduate from college or pay their taxes. As a self-employed yoga business owner, you must impose deadlines on your projects, or they'll never get done. Need to do a photo shoot? Put a date on the calendar and make it happen. Need to publish a YouTube video or work on a handout for an upcoming workshop? Schedule it, set a deadline, and hold yourself accountable. I will often announce my upcoming classes, workshops, or training events before I've even completed the planning phase. The moment I announce the date and start booking students, the pressure is on, and the work gets done. Most of us operate best with deadlines.

From ADD to Ultra-Organized

I know a yoga teacher named Benji who has severe ADD. In a single conversation, he'll jump to three different topics, get up from the table multiple times, and then apologize for it all. Before he taught yoga, he'd gotten fired from eleven different jobs, but somehow, when yoga class started, he was laser focused and present. It was remarkable to see the change. His ADD disappeared, and for an hour, he was a walking Buddha.

Once class finished, however, Benji immediately lost his focus and struggled to respond to emails or follow up on any client messages or projects. He was thirty-three years old at the time, his career was totally flatlining, and he was well aware that he was his own worst enemy. He'd watched younger teachers accelerate right past him, and even though he knew he was capable of more, he couldn't seem to get organized until he made a series of radical changes.

The first thing Benji did was get a second phone, a work phone. His work phone was a crappy, secondhand burner on which he installed Gmail, Google Calendar, and Google Maps—nothing else. During workdays, he left his other phone at home, only allowing himself access to his work phone. Next, he bought an external hard drive and did a data dump, moving every file on his computer to this external drive. After that, he reinstalled the operating system on his laptop so he had a fresh start. Last, he bought a desk with no drawers, so there was nowhere to hide papers or junk, and he made a rule for himself to clean off the desk completely every night before bed.

All of this sounds extreme, I know, but Benji had been teaching for over six years, and he'd yet to teach a single workshop, he'd never had a private client, and the only way he'd ever gotten paid as a yoga teacher was by teaching drop-in classes at the local studio. He was one of the best Rocket Yoga teachers in town, and yet he barely had enough money to pay his rent every month. His actions may have been extreme, but extreme is what he needed.

Benji still struggles with ADD of course, but after making these radical changes, he was able to increase his income by 30 percent the very next month and by 70 percent the following year. He did this primarily by adding private clients and workshops to his teaching portfolio, all of which he never would have been able to do without finding time and creating space for these new opportunities to unfold.

CHAPTER IX

Pricing and Packaging

During my first year of practice, I wanted to try every style of yoga possible. Om Yoga was a preeminent studio, located right on Union Square in New York City, and I'd seen a promotion offering new students three classes for thirty-nine dollars. Although I already had a membership at another studio, I figured I could take double classes a few days a week.

At the time, this whole yoga world was still new to me, and I felt like an oddball most of the time, worried that I'd be out of place. When I arrived on my first day, I was nervous that everyone else in the class would be better than me.

The line to sign up for class went out the door, so when I finally reached the desk, there were only a few minutes left before the start time. The receptionist said, "You're here for the six o'clock class, right?" I nodded. She charged me twenty-three dollars, the drop-in rate, and pointed me toward the changing rooms.

I took my first class with Beryl Bender Birch that day, and it was great. She taught a more mature and less militant version of Ashtanga Yoga than the other teachers I'd experienced. After class, I again thought about purchasing that three-class promotion, but the lobby was so busy that I had to ask people to move aside just to find my shoes. Flustered, I wiggled my way out the door and down onto the street.

Here's the rub. When I entered Om Yoga that day, I came prepared to spend thirty-nine dollars, and ninety minutes later, I left buzzing with excitement about the class. But I'd only spent twenty-three dollars. Worse still, it was nearly a year before I returned to the same studio, again for no good reason except that life got in the way. That receptionist made a huge mistake, albeit an extremely common one. Scenes like this play out every single day in yoga classes around the world. I'm the best type of yoga customer—I want everything—but when she only offered me one class, I followed her lead.

As the saying goes, "People need to pay to pay attention," and when it comes to health and fitness, a financial commitment is a huge part of a personal commitment. The class can be amazing, the teacher can be on point, and the student can be excited, but if the pricing and packaging is not strategic, students will walk away after class, just as I did.

As a teacher, you plan your sequences meticulously. You also need to plan your pricing to maximize the impact you have on your students and to grow your yoga business. There's a lot of content here, and it's important—pricing and packaging can make or break your success. However, these concepts can be overwhelming at first, so give yourself permission to digest this chapter in a piecemeal fashion, knowing you can always refer back to deepen your knowledge.

Avoid One-Off Classes

The first principle of effective pricing is simple: Never sell one-off classes. This is a golden rule, and in most circumstances, there's no reason to break it. It's not a money-hungry approach; instead, it's a strategic plan, based on what is best for both you and your students.

There are several reasons why this rule is important. First, students come to yoga seeking solutions to problems. If they suffer from stress, back pain, or lack of flexibility, one class is not going to solve that. Students intuitively know this. Second, as a teacher, you need job satisfaction. If your class is like a revolving door, with a constant intake of new students, you'll lose the gratification of seeing them progress and you'll become demotivated. Finally, from a business perspective, if you're focused on one-off classes, you'll waste huge amounts of time marketing and selling, time you'd rather spend teaching.

Many new teachers live hand to mouth and focus only on their next class, their next paycheck. If twenty-seven people come to class, they celebrate; if three people show up, they feel defeated. This boom-bust cycle of chasing short-term goals is exhausting, and it's not the way to build a real yoga business.

I have taught dozens of classes attended by just one or two students. I've also taught classes that were so big that they broke every record in the book. What I've come to learn is that if I plan my pricing for the long run, big or small, all classes are valuable. When you stop creating transactional relationships and instead start building your yoga community of members, I believe you'll experience the same mindset shift.

I first learned the value of membership in my early twenties, while working front of house in an off-off-Broadway theater. We sold tickets to single shows for twenty to fifty dollars, and that was fine, but we also served studio patrons, who subscribed for an entire season and paid hundreds of dollars for unlimited passes.

These subscribers came to every show, and the crew and I loved them. Why? They knew their way around the venue, arrived early, turned off their phones, and asked smart questions about the performers. These insiders were the best type of people to have in the audience. The random one-time visitors who showed up three minutes before curtain call were the source of most customer problems. The same principle applies in yoga.

Aim for a Triple Win

If you're not selling one-off classes, what should you do instead? How can you convince students to take a step that is undoubtedly in their best interests? Often, yoga teachers balk at this prospect. They are so uncomfortable talking about pricing that they fail to consider this concept. Instead, they set a flat per-class rate and say, "Come if you want; here's how much it costs." I understand their frustration, but that approach is not in the best interest of anyone. When it comes to money and yoga business, you need to optimize for what I call the *triple win.*

The first win is always focused on your students. In order for you to succeed as a teacher, your students need to get results and grow in their practices. This is non-negotiable. The second win refers to your job satisfaction. The teaching experience itself must be rewarding and meaningful, or you'll get bored and burn out. I used to teach wedding parties, for example, but I'll never do that again. The attendees loved it; I hated it. The third win refers to your bank account. You need to receive a fee commensurate with the value of your services. If you're underpaid, long-term you'll grow resentful and bitter.

When you apply this triple-win paradigm, it becomes much easier to analyze your pricing and teaching opportunities. Will this be a win for my students? Is this something I'll find worthwhile? Is this going to grow my bank account? If the answer is yes to all three, you have a green light to proceed. If you're getting one or more no responses, you should probably reconsider.

The Power of Introductory Offers

Once you've established the triple-win philosophy, how can you move students toward doing the things that will result in a triple win? Initially, almost every student will inquire about purchasing a single class. This is normal, but we've established that it won't result in a triple win; it's not in anyone's best interest. Instead of simply selling students a single class, here is what you should do. First, make your single classes comparatively expensive to discourage people from buying them. Second, create a low-cost introductory offer to serve as an obvious, more attractive alternative.

The number one reason students want to buy a single class in the first place is because they are unsure whether you or your classes are right for them—they're nervous, just like I was walking into Om Yoga! To bridge this gap and to lower the barriers to entry, introductory offers are a mainstay of the yoga business.

What does an introductory offer look like? Sometimes it's one week of unlimited yoga for twenty-nine dollars, or your first three classes for twenty-nine dollars. There are lots of different ways to structure an introductory offer, and different price points will be appropriate in different markets. As a rule of thumb, the intro offer should cost less than the price of two drop-in classes, and your objective is to encourage students to take at least three classes as quickly as possible.

To illustrate how this plays out in reality, imagine a student messages you online and wants to sign up for the class you're teaching tonight.

Student: *I saw you have a Power Yoga class tonight at seven o'clock. Is it still possible to join?*

You: *Yes! We still have space. Shall I save a mat for you?*

Student: *Great! How much is the class? Can I pay online?*

You: *The class is twenty-three dollars, but what most people do is sign up for my new-student offer where you get three classes for twenty-nine dollars. This way, you can try a few classes, meet some students, and decide if it's right for you.*

Student: *Great. Let's do the three classes.*

In this scenario, students will join your introductory offer over 80 percent of the time. Why? Because it's a no-brainer. It's a great value, and they already know they need more than one class, so it just makes sense. "What most people do" is a very useful phrase here, because when we're new to something, we generally want to follow the crowd—at least at first.

Amateur teachers often get nervous about intro offers and protest, "At that rate, I'm charging less than ten dollars per class! That's too cheap." Here's the reality. Without the introductory offer, your prospective student might have spent only twenty-three dollars; with it, they are spending twenty-nine dollars—that's a 26 percent increase right away. It doesn't cost you any more to have another student in your classes, so there's nothing lost, only gained. Remember, your goal is to help students and to create long-term relationships, and this offer makes both much more likely.

CHOOSE YOUR INTRODUCTORY OFFER

Not all introductory offers are created equal. Some pave the way for fulfilling long-term relationships with your students, whereas others set low-cost expectations you're unable to sustain. It's essential that your introductory offer establishes a price that is both attractive in the short term and sustainable over the long term. Most teachers miss this important detail. Consumers hate bait-and-switch pricing, where they get a good deal initially but then face steep increases later. Your goal is to offer a great deal today and then continue with the same rates—or better—for future purchases.

Here's how this works. If your introductory offer is three classes for twenty-nine dollars, for example, you've established a value of about ten dollars per class. To keep this offer going long term, after the introductory offer expires, you simply ask for a bigger commitment, such as a ten-class purchase. Here's how your full pricing structure might look:

- Intro Special x3 Classes = Just $29*
- 1 class = $16
- 4-class pack = $49
- 10-class pack = $99

One time only, new students only, one-week validity

MEMBERSHIP MODEL INTRO OFFERS

The membership pricing model is a variation on the introductory offer. If you control all your class payments and if you teach at least four days per week, I'd encourage you to offer an unlimited intro offer instead of a class pack. Unlimited offers represent a great value to students and allow them to feel like a member right away. Your goal, as the teacher, is to encourage them to take at least three classes—and even more if they can—during their intro period.

Unlimited Intro Offer Options:
- One Week Unlimited = $X
- Ten Days Unlimited = $X
- Twenty-One Days Unlimited = $X
- Thirty Days Unlimited = $X

Your immediate goal should be to quickly turn those intro students into longer-term members or class cardholders. Imagine your intro week is $29 and your monthly membership is $119. You can offer your student a $29 credit if they upgrade to a monthly membership during their intro week.

Alternatively, perhaps you're using a three-class introductory special for $29. You can offer students three extra classes if they book a ten-class card during their first week. Remember, now is always the best time. The longer your students wait, the greater the chances they will get distracted by other non-health-related activities in their lives. Help them commit to themselves when their enthusiasm is highest.

INTRO OFFERS: COMMON QUESTIONS

Introductory offers look simple, but it's easy to overlook the strategy behind this approach. Below are answers to questions and doubts that often arise when I teach pricing to instructors.

Q: *What if a student really can only attend one class? What if they are traveling or just visiting?*

A: *Sell them just one class. Your objective is not to be rigid, but you do want to be strategic.*

Q: *What if students abuse my unlimited introductory offer and come to every single class?*

A: *That is not abuse; that is a raving fan. Welcome them happily to every class, stop counting short-term revenue, and think long term. This student will become your ambassador.*

Q: *What if a student doesn't use all the classes in their introductory offer?*

A: *If they don't use it, they lose it. Time pressure is important, or students will never follow through. Three-class intro offers are usually valid for seven days, and one-week unlimited offers are valid for seven consecutive days. Be strict about the validity or the intro offer will be useless.*

Q: *What if a student wants to keep buying the introductory offer again and again?*

A: *Disallow this. Intro offers are for first-time students only, but make sure you have an equally good package offer that simply requires a larger commitment (see example above).*

More Is Not More, Cheap Is Not Valued

Time limitation is a key component of the introductory offer. I once offered a hugely discounted three-month introductory offer. It was a great deal, so it was wildly popular, but because the time period was so long, most students didn't even make it to three classes during the entire ninety-day period. Worse still, after their trial, most students never came back. It seemed like they were getting incredible value—and they could have—but in practice, most didn't. It was a long way from being a triple win.

The psychology of health and fitness can be very counterintuitive. We want and need some pressure to follow through. If given the opportunity, many of us will simply procrastinate and delay, instead of showing up to class. More time is not always more value. Your intro offer should be short, with a limited validity period.

Although you want to offer great value, don't make the mistake of attempting to compete through low prices. If you own a gas station, low prices will work. In yoga, cheap prices often have the opposite effect. Unconsciously, the low-price leader is often associated with low quality.

Years ago, my staff got really excited about a tiny yoga studio around the corner from our office. They took classes together on their lunch breaks. I loved the idea, so I started paying for the classes myself to encourage them to keep it up. Then something weird happened.

The studio was struggling financially (as most do) and decided to position itself as the low-price leader. They cut their class prices so low that some classes were as cheap as four dollars. The result? My staff stopped going! Remember, the classes got cheaper, not more expensive, and remember, I was the one paying. Why did they care?

When it comes to our own health and wellness, very few of us want the lowest-quality option; in fact, many of us want the best we can afford. With that in mind, aim to be competitive in your market but never the cheapest option.

Now Is Always the Best Time to Decide

Our purchasing behaviors are often driven by a sense of urgency. Although we tend to think of urgency as a negative thing, positive urgency such as "I want to do this right now!" is just as powerful. When it comes to purchasing decisions, our willingness to commit is at its peak early in an experience, when we're most excited—often during that very first visit.

That first day I attended Om Yoga Studio, for example, I was primed and ready for more, but no one offered me anything. The following day, my enthusiasm had waned. Not because I changed my mind about the studio or had second thoughts; my focus had simply gone someplace else. There are so many things constantly vying for our attention, so always remember that now is the best time to offer your student a package.

In a theoretical world, students would take a yoga class, go home, read some yoga books, research on Google, and then decide which path they would follow for the next year. In reality, our lives unfold as the result of a series of small decisions, which collectively set us down a new path. A student's first yoga class is one of those potential forks in the road. Don't wait. Offer them an opportunity to go further, and offer it right away.

Two of my earliest students were a couple named Mike and Apple who lived just down the street. Mike contacted me initially via email, and then I met the two of them to talk about my classes.

I told the couple about my introductory unlimited week of yoga, but right away, they asked if I had a yearlong membership. I didn't, but I told them, "Yes, of course!" and ten minutes later, I signed them up for a year's worth of classes.

Keep in mind, Mike and Apple hadn't taken a single class before making that decision—not from me or anyone. Why did they want to make such a large purchase? It was January, they had set some goals for themselves, and they wanted to take action. Quickly, they became two of my best students, attending evening classes three or four nights a week. These types of stories occur all the time in yoga, but they don't happen by accident. If you want them to happen to you, you need to set up your offers in a way that invites new students to dive in headfirst.

Recurring Revenue Is Queen

Let's assume that you have a paying client who is happy and ready to deepen their relationship with you. What should you do next? Whenever possible, give students an opportunity to pay monthly. Many of the important purchases in our lives are paid through monthly recurring billing: your rent or mortgage payment, your electric bill, your music subscription, and your video streaming services. As a yoga teacher, if at all possible, you'll want to give your students the opportunity to add your classes to their list of regular monthly expenses.

If you teach in a studio or fitness center, they surely offer monthly recurring billing already. If you're an independent teacher, you can often find creative ways to offer monthly memberships as well. Let's imagine your teaching schedule looks like this:

- Tuesday and Thursday: one-hour evening virtual class (via Zoom)
- Saturday: outdoor morning class in the park
- Friday: two-hour class at a rented dance studio
- Workshop: one Sunday afternoon per month at the same dance studio

In total, you offer four weekly classes and one monthly workshop. Most teachers with a schedule like this would simply sell class packs—and that's smart—but you should also consider a monthly rate: something like sixty-nine dollars for an all-access pass to every class and workshop. The exact number is up to you—you'll need to do the math to determine whether this price point works for you and your area—but the principle is universal. The idea is to make it at least 50 percent less expensive for your students to have full access to every class and workshop you teach than it is for them to pay class by class.

Why do this? The psychological shift that happens once your students are "all in" with you for the month is palpable. They become better students, creating a win-win-win situation. Better still, once students have made a commitment for one month, they no longer have to decide whether to continue; they can set up a monthly payment with auto-billing. Remember, it's rare that unlimited members actually come to every class, but they love the option that they can.

TIP: the simplest way to set up auto-billing is with PayPal subscriptions.

Understand Crowd Pricing

When you set up your monthly subscription options, you should offer three tiers: low cost, medium, and VIP. In every industry, there are big spenders, bargain hunters, and then the vast majority in the middle. As an example, let's talk about sneakers. At a big-box retailer like Walmart, you could easily buy a pair of sports shoes for around $30. They would be off-brand and not the best quality, but they are available, and people buy them every day.

At a traditional shoe retailer, an average pair of sports shoes might cost $60–$100, and these are the ones most people buy. The quality is good, the price is not too expensive, and the purchase seems like a decent value. A small percentage of people, however, will visit specialty stores and websites, where they'll spend $100, $200, or even $300+ on a pair of sneakers.

Why does this happen? It's because we all value things differently. For most people, $350 is an outrageous amount of money to spend on shoes. For a sneakerhead, it's totally worth it. They'll spend cheaply on other things in their life but happily drain their bank account to pick up a sweet new pair of kicks. This principle is true in any market, including yoga. Broadly speaking, the numbers break down like this:

- Ten percent of people will choose the cheapest option.
- Eighty percent of people will purchase something in the midrange.
- Ten percent will choose the most expensive offer.

High spenders are often referred to as whales, and in the yoga market, I'm a whale. Even when I barely had enough money to pay my rent, I had the best yoga mat, multiple yoga memberships, and

I went to every workshop I could find. In almost all other areas of my life, I'm frugal; I own very little. But with all things yoga, I'm a dream customer. Annual memberships, oversized yoga mats, travel bags, books, and pose charts—I want them all. Don't attempt to change crowd purchasing psychology; instead, understand and utilize it in your business to create relevant offers for your clients.

Make Your Prices Pretty

In the same way strategic pricing options make your offers more appealing, the number itself also plays a role in your clients' decisions. As crazy as it sounds, the way your numbers look can make a big difference in their appeal, and you'll see proof of this everywhere. When you go to the grocery store, you'll find laundry detergent for $9.99, not $13; $13 is ugly. You might find pears on offer for $2.99 per pound, but not $3.17 per pound. We all know that $2.99 is barely different from $3, and yet we perceive $2.99 as lower cost and better value. In business, these small details matter.

When you create your prices, make sure your numbers are attractive, not clunky. This often means rounding down or rounding up. Let's imagine your intro offer is three classes for $29. That's a pretty number. But what if your intro offer was $33? That's just weird and looks much more expensive. Here are examples of some pricing strategies to avoid (ugly prices) and some to follow (pretty prices):

Ugly Prices:
- Intro Special: Unlimited classes for one week $33
- $62 access to unlimited online classes
- $71 access to unlimited online classes + all in-person classes
- $136 all of the above + one private class per month

Pretty Prices:
- Intro Special: Unlimited classes for one week $29
- $59 access to unlimited online classes
- $69 access unlimited online classes + all in-person classes
- $129 all of the above + one private class per month

In the above pretty price example, most people will choose the $69 offer. Some people will opt for the cheapest option, which is expected, and a small minority will buy the biggest offer. In almost every case and in every market, the big spenders and the cheap buyers balance each other out, while those in the middle account for the bulk of purchases. Your assignment is to always make sure you have a compelling introductory offer and three pricing tiers available for different types of buyers.

Transparent Pricing

When you apply the principles described in this chapter, you will have the occasional student who questions your prices with probing questions such as, "Why are you charging more than the gym?" "Why don't you offer classes on Sundays?" "Why is your drop-in class so expensive?"

The fitness industry has a bad reputation for sneaky pricing tricks and binding long-term contracts. At one time in life, most people have been stuck paying for a gym membership they never use. As a yoga teacher, you have an opportunity to reverse this perception. The more you can operate your business with full transparency and no tricks, the happier your customers will be.

Pricing conversations scare many teachers, but as long as you are transparent and well intentioned, there is no reason to worry. Here are some common price discussions, all of which are easy to manage when you're completely transparent.

Q: *"Why is your intro offer twenty-nine dollars instead of thirty dollars? Why don't you just make it thirty dollars?"*

A: *"I know it's silly, but for whatever reason, twenty-nine dollars is more popular than thirty dollars. I lose a dollar, but I gain a student."*

Q: *"Why is your class rate higher than my personal trainer?"*

A: *"I'd love to be able to match your personal trainer's rates, but I'm not able to operate at that price."*

Q: *"Why can't I just pay class by class? Why do I have to purchase a package?"*

A: *"I've found that when people prepay for class packages, they show up to classes more often and get better results, which is better for them and for me."*

Q: *"Why can't I just keep buying the introductory offer? That's a better deal."*

A: *"The intro offer is just for new students, but my ten-session pack is exactly the same price per class as the intro offer, so I'd recommend that one."*

Q: *"Why is your single-class rate so high?"*

A: *"I price single classes high so people don't buy them. As a teacher, it's most rewarding for me to see students learn and grow, and I can't help them do that with just one class. The intro offer is a better deal."*

How to Get Paid like a Professional

Throughout this book, we've emphasized the importance of professionalism. You want to earn the respect and benefits enjoyed by top-tier service providers. One surefire way to undermine your credibility is to ask for cash instead of card payments. Many yoga teachers try to operate cash-only businesses, but this almost guarantees you'll never earn a good salary. Cash is dying fast and will soon be completely obsolete. Your goal is to serve clients who spend hundreds of dollars with you, but no one carries that much cash with them anymore.

Yes, this means you'll have to pay merchant fees and taxes. This is part of owning a grown-up business, and it's often offset by an immediate increase in income. I know many teachers who achieved a 25–30 percent income increase the very first month they switched to digital payments. Your clients don't want to drive to the cash machine so you can dodge taxes. Don't ask them to, or you'll end up losing them.

Popular options for online payments:
- PayPal.com*
- Venmo/peer-to-peer payments
- Stripe
- Square

*PayPal purchase links can be easily added to your personalized Bio Page at www.YogaBody.bio.

Special Circumstances Pricing

As you've learned, structured strategic pricing is a key to success, but there are always exceptions—and this should be expected. When the need arises, be willing to negotiate special packages. Perhaps one of your regular students asks if she can bring her out-of-town friend to one of your classes. Don't be so rigid that you refuse to sell her a single class. If one student splits her time between two different cities and is only in town for half the month, you might create a special 50-percent-off package just for her.

When students request a special membership or special deal, my go-to answer is, "Thanks for your interest. Let me think about that, and I'll get back to you." It's important to give myself the time and space to do some math and make sure that I can offer something fair to me, fair to the student, and also fair to my existing members. Students will talk among themselves, and if they become aware of preferential treatment, their trust in you will be broken.

When people push back against your pricing or ask for a special deal, it's important to remember that they're not saying they don't want to work with you. If they were truly uninterested, they would walk out the door. Usually, students negotiating rates are trying to work out a solution that aligns with their head and their wallet. If you can stay calm, answer their questions fairly, and maintain transparency, you can usually find a way to create a win-win-win scenario.

Pricing and Packaging Is Not Sales

Many teachers instinctively resist pricing and packaging discussions. They don't think of themselves as salespeople or marketers. For many, an aversion to this aspect of business is part of what motivated them to teach yoga instead of climbing the corporate ladder. The good news is that you don't need to learn complex sales skills or marketing tactics to successfully sell your yoga classes. If you manage your pricing and packaging well, your yoga classes will sell themselves, especially when you focus on creating win-win-win scenarios.

Almost no one likes selling, and no one enjoys being sold to, but everyone enjoys making good value purchases that meet their needs over time. The goal with your pricing and packaging is to create attractive, compelling, high-value offers for your students. The goal is not for you to manipulate people but simply to make it easy for people to make a financial commitment toward their health and wellness.

Six-Week Career Makeover

I had a student named Jay who taught yoga, dance fitness, and personal training in New York City. He was doing well for himself, but since his entire life was focused on charging session by session, he was constantly working, constantly chasing new clients, and unable to predict his earnings.

One month, he'd make $6,000, and the next month he might make $4,000. He often worked seven days per week, and he'd take bookings at any time because he was worried that if he missed an earning opportunity, he might not be able to meet his financial needs.

Jay came to me because he wanted to learn how to build a great website and market himself online. I told him to forget all that and instead work on his pricing and packaging. We made a rule: no one-off classes. We sat down and mapped out one-month, two-month, and three-month prepaid training programs that involved Jay going to his clients' homes to train them once per week.

We went back and forth for about an hour until we found the price points that we thought would be most appropriate. We included an option for the low-end buyers, an option for the high-end buyers, and a mid-range offer, which we assumed most people would prefer.

Many of Jay's clients had practiced with him for years, so he was nervous to announce the change, but he did it. And it worked. Over the next six weeks, Jay earned more than five times what he'd normally make as he presold his schedule far into the future. His clients were more than happy to prepay, as he offered them great prices. Suddenly, Jay knew exactly what his workweek would look like and exactly how much he'd earn.

His social life improved, he stopped taking weekend and late-night work, and he finally enjoyed the stability and security he deserved. Jay was already successful as a teacher, but his pricing failures were destroying his quality of life. Once he fixed his pricing and packaging, Jay was finally able to enjoy the successful business he'd built. I should also mention that Jay gave up his plans to improve his website and learn digital marketing. He didn't need to. He was booked up twelve to sixteen weeks in advance, with a waiting list for new clients. This is the power of strategic pricing in action.

CHAPTER X

Your Online Profile

In 2017, I interviewed a woman named Kay for a teaching position. She had a great résumé and positive energy, and she led an excellent test class. My team and I were excited about the possibility of adding her to our staff—that is, until I did a Google search on her name. As I'm sure you know, this is standard practice. Every employer does a due diligence web search on potential hires to look for green lights or red flags.

In the yoga industry, a green light is an online profile that illustrates an applicant's interest and experience in yoga. Red flags include inappropriate photos, hate speech, and obvious warning signs like a criminal record. When I searched Kay's name, her Instagram profile popped up as the number one search result, and it was filled with nude photos, albeit with blurred-out sections to get around the platform's adult content filters.

I have no idea what Kay does outside of yoga, and honestly, it should be none of my business. Unfortunately, by publishing public photos like that, it suddenly became my business. In the same way I Googled her name, students will do the same.

Reluctantly, we had to pass on hiring Kay, and the decision came down to those pictures. This is not fair to her, and it's not appropriate for me to judge anyone's (legal) behavior, and yet I do judge. We all make judgments, for better or worse, and I simply didn't want my students to find her online profile.

Think of your online profile like the clothes you might choose to wear for a job interview. In an ideal world, you should be able to wear whatever you want. In the real world, you need to look the part.

Kay's profile was an extreme example, but many teachers' online profiles are filled with photos of them drinking, sexually explicit photos, and even photos of illegal drug use. There are also many teachers with no online profile at all, and that too is usually a mistake.

In the end, I'm sure that Kay found a teaching job and is doing just fine, but I'm also sure that she's been passed over dozens of times for opportunities because she didn't take two minutes to change her Instagram settings to private before applying for the job.

In this chapter, I'll walk you through some simple ways you can quickly present yourself online as the yoga teaching professional that you are. Just as you might carefully pick out an outfit for an interview, you should take time to shape your online image appropriately as well.

Perform a Social Media Cleanup

Before you build or add to your existing online profile, you should start with a cleanup. This is best done with a friend looking over your shoulder, as they will often spot red flags you might overlook. You don't need to overanalyze every post, but do pay special attention to your photo and video content. Ask yourself: What if my student or boss saw this post? What would they think? Is this controversial? Appropriate?

If you find a post that is potentially inappropriate, you can delete it, archive it, or change privacy settings to friends only.

Choose whichever option is best for you. Don't overthink this process; simply scroll through your feed and clean it up. If you're in a rush, you can also switch your entire account to private. This is probably not the best long-term strategy, but if you're pressed for time, it's an acceptable quick fix.

Do a Google Cleanup

Google search your name and click on any links or references that show up on the first page. If you find something that might be a red flag for a potential employer, change it, or do your best to bury it.

I have a colleague who was arrested during a political rally years ago, and when people searched his name, the incident appeared on two news sites. He attended a peaceful protest for an environmental cause, but when his group crossed onto private property (a farm), they were all arrested. In his small town, the event was significant enough to make the news and those four-year-old articles continued to haunt him. The articles were not scandalous or damning in any way, but still, the optics were bad.

My colleague asked the news sites to remove the stories, but they didn't bother to respond. To his credit, he came up with a clever solution that can work for you too. He wrote articles for two different yoga websites, and he created one educational YouTube video. His goal was to "crowd out" the bad news with new content, and it worked.

Within three weeks, this new content bumped the news stories off the first page of Google and essentially buried them. He wasn't trying to cover up a murder; he simply wanted to give himself the best chance for employment. People will judge you. Small things matter, so do your best to clean up anything potentially problematic.

Your Assignment:
- Google search your name and look for red flags.
- Try to remove any red flags you can.
- If removal is not possible, try to crowd out red flags with new online content.

Be Visible Online

Although inappropriate or controversial content is a problem for many yoga teachers, these kinds of red flags are not nearly as common as invisibility. Invisibility occurs when your employers, partners, or teachers search your name and find nothing at all. It's not a red flag, but it's also not helpful. You already know people will search your name, so why not give them something to find? If you're starting from scratch, you can quickly create Google-friendly references using some of the following:

YOGABODY.BIO

Set up a free bio page using this free tool I created for you and other yoga teachers (use access code: ytcalumni). This takes only a few minutes, and your page will start to appear in Google search results within a week or two.

LINKEDIN.COM

This is not a popular site among yoga teachers, but it ranks well in Google and is a simple and free way to promote your name in search results. Spend fifteen minutes and create an up-to-date profile.

YOUTUBE.COM

Create a simple "about me" video to introduce yourself and your teaching. Share this on YouTube with your name in the title, and it will often pop up on the first page of Google. This video is not intended to attract maximum views; the purpose is to plant your flag online and build an online presence.

ARTICLES

Write yoga articles for websites such as HuffPost.com or Medium. com, and they will often rank on Google when people search your name. Choose a topic related to your style of yoga and share some of your best ideas. Articles can take months to rank, but when they do, they last for years and help you establish authority.

How to Write Your Yoga Biography

As a yoga teacher, you'll need to create a biography that can be used on studio websites, on social media, and in future promotional materials. Trying to capture your story in a pithy paragraph can feel daunting, but I have a very simple three-step structure that makes it easy.

It's helpful to have both a first- and third-person biography to use in different settings. This biography will usually end up 150–200 words long and is appropriate for websites, long-form social media bios, and promotional materials.

STEP I: Share your before and after yoga story.

[First-Person Example] Before I discovered yoga, I was your typical stressed-out office worker. My back pain got so bad that I had to stand up every hour at work just to relieve the tension. Back pain is what drove me to my first class, but what I found was a holistic mind–body practice that soon influenced every aspect of my life.

[Third-Person Example] Before Jay discovered yoga, he was your typical stressed-out office worker. His back pain got so bad that he had to stand up every hour at work just to relieve the tension. Back pain is what drove Jay to his first class, but what he found was a holistic mind–body practice that soon influenced every aspect of his life.

STEP II: Share your professional journey as a teacher.

[First-Person Example] My yoga practice quickly became the highlight of my day, and I found myself less and less interested in my office job in marketing. Just a year after I started my practice, I was certified to teach, and over a period of six months, I phased out my previous working life and embraced an entirely new focus as a full-time yoga teacher. Today, I specialize in

alignment-based yoga for spinal health and rehabilitation. I teach all ages and all body types, and the goal of my classes is to help you live pain-free and mobile well into later life.

[Third-Person Example] Jay's yoga practice quickly became the highlight of his day, and he found himself less and less interested in his office job in marketing. Just a year after he started his practice, he was certified to teach, and over a period of six months, he phased out his previous work life and embraced an entirely new focus as a full-time yoga teacher. Today, he specializes in alignment-based yoga for spinal health and rehabilitation. He teaches all ages and all body types, and the goal of his classes is to help you live pain-free and mobile well into later life.

STEP III: Invite students to your class.

[First-Person Example] I teach private classes both in person and virtually, and my weekly group classes are held at Starwood Community Center. If you're struggling with back pain or if you simply want to experience the spine-healing benefits of yoga, I invite you to join my classes.

[Third-Person Example] Jay teaches private classes both in person and virtually, and his weekly group classes are held at Starwood Community Center. If you're struggling with back pain or if you simply want to experience the spine-healing benefits of yoga, Jay invites you to join his classes.

DOS AND DON'TS OF BIOGRAPHY WRITING

Do be clear, concise, and accurate.
Don't brag, exaggerate, or try to impress.

Do use conversational, grammatically correct language.
Don't try to be cute, silly, or funny.

Do share your real-world experiences and knowledge.
Don't try to fit some yogi stereotype that is not true to you.

Do share relevant, related interests such as other movement practices, bodywork, health, and nutrition.
Don't include references to your dog, your favorite coffee, or other irrelevant things.

Do share your approach to yoga.
Don't criticize other styles of yoga or approaches.

Do inject your bio with your personal energy.
Don't quote Rumi, Gandhi, or Mother Teresa (it's cliché).

SHORT-FORM BIOGRAPHIES

Many social media platforms, such as Instagram and TikTok, restrict your bio section to just a sentence or two. Since this is not enough room to present any real biographical details, it's best to share your unique teaching positioning (covered in Chapter III) instead.

Examples of effective short-form biographies:

If you're struggling with anxiety and overwhelm, I teach Yoga for Inner Peace, a meditative class for balance and whole-person wellness.

If you're a triathlete with constant injuries, I teach a Tri-Yoga class specifically to lengthen and heal overtrained athletes' bodies.

If you're over the age of sixty-five and want to regain the energy and mobility of someone ten years younger, then my Golden Years Yoga class is for you.

If you're a runner struggling with knee pain, I teach Yoga for Pain-Free Running on Saturdays in the park.

Yoga for New Mothers. I teach postpartum yoga for pelvic-floor rehab, prolapse, diastasis recti, and incontinence.

If you're struggling with overwhelm and anxiety, I teach Stress Less Yoga to help you regain balance and peace. DM me for free Discovery Class.

If you have stiff hamstrings, locked-up hips, and a painful lower back, my Yoga for Mobility classes are here to help. First class free.

If you love a hot and sweaty yoga class, I teach a Fitness Flow class weekdays at XYZ Studio. Beginner special $29 x3 classes.

If you're recovering from a back, knee, shoulder, or other joint injury, I teach private, custom rehab classes. Free Discovery Class.

Yoga is for everybody. Join my Body Love yoga classes on Tues and Thurs evenings at XYZ Yoga. First class free.

If you suffer from chronic lower back pain, my Happy Back weekly workshop can help. All levels, all ages. DM me for an intro special.

Stay Sane on Social Media

Many people have a love-hate relationship with social media. It helps you connect to friends and family, inspires you, and enrages you all at the same time. For most yoga teachers, social media is an essential tool, but you run the risk of getting sucked into the vortex. We can all agree that appropriate use of social media is a complicated subject.

From a professional perspective, there are a few reasons you should consider social media profiles. First, it's a way for you to claim a little piece of real estate online and build your professional profile. Second, your students are on social media all day long, so it makes sense to meet them there. Last, social media can be a great way to build and grow a community.

Over the years, my activity on social media has waxed and waned. There was a period when I posted multiple times per day and shared every little thing that happened in my personal and professional life. Now I hardly ever post, and I actively unfollow, block, and time-regulate my personal use of these apps.

How should you use social media? There is no right answer for all. Everyone must determine appropriate use for themselves, but I'd like to give you permission to ignore all the social media gurus and their advice. Those people spend their entire day working on the perfect photo or video they hope will go viral. That's probably not how you want to spend your time.

Whatever you decide, remember the yoga business is about *you* and *your community*, so any time you invest in social media should help build one or both of those assets. Everything else is a distraction.

INSTAGRAM

Currently, Instagram is the most popular social media site for yoga students and teachers. Even if you're mostly inactive like me, you should still set up a professional profile, add some posts to your feed, and most importantly, answer your direct messages. Every business owner should be delighted to have their customers contacting them, and remember, every direct message is one of your students raising their hand and asking to be part of your community.

Your profile:

- **Photo.** Choose a recent, close-up headshot. Make sure your eyes are clearly visible to make you personable and real.

- **Name.** Use your real name here, as students will go directly to the app and type in your name after class.

- **Category.** Choose "yoga teacher" or "fitness instructor" or "local business." Not everyone has the same options in their accounts, so choose the available category that best describes you.

- **Bio Text.** You get 150 characters, so use this area to share your unique teaching positioning (see example above).

- **Link.** Make sure to include a link. YOGABODY.bio is a great option, as you can customize it to add all your details, and it's free.

If your Instagram feed lacks yoga content, start with a total of nine posts. When in doubt, focus on educational content. Share the tips and tricks you teach in class that are most helpful to your students in a series of photo or video posts. If you try to impress or go viral, you'll get stuck. If you focus on education, you'll know exactly what to share and you'll know that at the very least, you're adding value to your followers.

FACEBOOK

Facebook has grown into a monster. It's very difficult to use, and yet billions of people use it daily. It's not the most popular social media site for yoga people, but it is used in lieu of a website for millions of small businesses. Since a Facebook Business Page is an important piece of online real estate, you should claim yours and invest some time in the setup.

Best practices:
- Copy your profile photos, bio, and other settings from Instagram.
- Add a cover photo that shows you teaching or practicing yoga. Be sure it's nothing extreme. Share a teaching or pose photo that looks professional.
- If you teach in a physical location, be sure to add your telephone number, address, and other relevant contact details. Students often trust contact information from Facebook more than websites for local businesses.
- Copy your feed posts from Instagram onto Facebook.
- Many students will contact you via Facebook Messenger, so be sure to check your messages regularly.

LINKEDIN

In the yoga world, LinkedIn is not so popular, but as discussed earlier, it ranks very well in Google for your name, so invest the time to set up a professional profile. Be sure to include all your past work experiences, including non-yoga jobs. Your potential employers and students will be interested in your background, and you'll be surprised how often your non-yoga background will open doors for future yoga work. Use the same profile photos and bio here, but don't bother posting anything to your feed.

YOUTUBE

YouTube is not a true social media platform; it's a publishing platform. The social element is minimal and mostly consists of random comments under videos. YouTube as a platform is extremely powerful, but it's a lot of work. Most yoga teachers have no interest in becoming YouTubers, but I still recommend you set up an account for two reasons. First, as described earlier, you should post an "about me" video where you introduce yourself and your teaching online. Second, you should have a YouTube account since it's a great way to share unlisted and private videos with your clients.

Use the same profile picture as before, and simply copy your biography as well. On YouTube, you can link to all your other web profiles on your "about" page, so take advantage of this facility. What about becoming a yoga YouTuber? Although it is possible to earn ad revenue from YouTube as a content creator, at the time of this writing, there are fewer than two dozen yoga creators in the world making significant money on the platform. It can be done, but it's challenging.

TIKTOK

TikTok is still finding its feet among the yoga community, and it's unclear as yet whether there is an opportunity to build community or teach on the platform. If you are interested in creating short-form creative videos, there is an extremely active audience in this app, so test it out! If you use your real name as your TikTok name, it will often appear in Google search results. TikTok's community is very strong, but it remains very challenging for you to build your own community on the platform.

TRADE SITES AND DIRECTORIES

When people search your name, they will find anywhere from zero to ten results on their search page, so why not claim more of that available real estate by adding yourself to trade sites and local listings sites? Even clumsy, outdated web directories can rank very well and receive lots of traffic, particularly in local markets.

Where to list yourself:

- **YOGABODY.bio.** Once you set up a bio page, your name and page will automatically be listed in the YOGABODY Teacher Directory. This is offered free for all readers. Use code: ytcalumni.

- **Yoga Alliance.** If you are registered with any of the Yoga Alliance organizations, be sure to complete your profile and take the time to make your listing look professional.

- **Directory Sites.** Many cities and towns have service directories where service providers can register. If you find another place to plant your flag, do it! These listings can often live on for years and help you further establish your profile.

GOOGLE BUSINESS PROFILE (GOOGLE MAPS)

If you have a fixed retail location, setting up a Google Business Profile can be a great way to show up in search results. Business profiles look amazing in search results, as they include location, photos, reviews, contact information, and hours of operation. For many teachers, this won't be relevant, but if you do teach at a fixed location, Google Business Profiles are a great tool for adding authority to your business via search results.

Wait to Build a Website

A teacher I know, named Steve, spent five years creating a fantastic website. He was a photographer turned yoga teacher, so he wanted to capture his yoga journey in a series of epic photos and stories. It was a beautiful project, and I remember thinking "wow" the first time I saw it.

Unfortunately, by the time his site went live, the code the developer had used was obsolete, the images were huge and slow, and it cost him fifty dollars per hour simply to update his teaching schedule. To this day, that beautiful, clunky website sits online, useless, with almost no traffic. Steve gets upset if I even ask about it, and he has switched to using Instagram to connect with his students.

When I started my career, all serious teachers invested in websites. Today, because online activity has changed, some of the top teachers I know don't bother at all. Students rarely spend time on their teacher's websites; instead, they spend time on social media apps, either engaging with general content or directly with their teachers. Websites are a hassle to set up and update, so unless there's a clear need for you to have a site, my suggestion is that you invest your time in your social media profiles.

Perfectionism Is a Myth

My excuse for waiting to set up my profiles was that I wanted perfect photos, a better bio, and more compelling content. I told people that I was a perfectionist, but I've come to learn that "I'm a perfectionist" is actually code for "I'm scared." I was scared to put myself online, receive nasty comments, and open myself up to judgment. I'm not going to tell you your fears are completely unjustified, but I will tell you to do it anyway. No one is perfect; waiting doesn't make it any easier. So stop procrastinating, and take action.

From Horses to Yoga

A few years ago, I worked with Bettina, a horse trainer turned yoga teacher. When people searched her name, there were dozens of photos, articles, awards, and references, but it was all about horses. Bettina wanted to leave her professional work with horses and rebrand herself as a yoga teacher, and she managed to make the switch with only four hours of work on a Saturday.

First, she switched all her horse-related social media accounts to private. She didn't lose any of her past posts or contacts, but now she could very easily position her yoga life more prominently online. Next, Bettina created new online profiles under the name *Yoga with Bettina*. Last, she created a photo-tutorial article titled "Stretches for Horseback Riders" and used contacts from her previous job to get it published on two different websites.

Within a week, Bettina's YOGABODY Bio Page and social media accounts were on the first page of Google. The articles took about three weeks to show up in the search results, but by the end of the month, it was clear to anyone looking that Bettina was a yoga teacher with an equestrian background—exactly what she wanted to convey.

A non-yoga-related profile is not a red flag, nor is it a green light. It would be wonderful if everyone you worked with gave careful consideration, in-depth interviews, and a chance for you to share who you really are. In the real world, we're all pressed for time, so employers, clients, and potential partners make snap judgments based on very limited information. Knowing this, it makes sense to invest some time, like Bettina, and present yourself in the best possible way.

CHAPTER XI

Get the Gig

After teaching in Bangkok for a while, I got the travel bug again. Hong Kong was dubbed the New York City of Asia, so experiencing it became my new obsession. Since moving to Hong Kong would nearly double my cost of living, I couldn't afford to just turn up and hope for the best. I needed a job, a work visa, and a place to live. The only option was to execute my entire plan from Thailand.

My online search uncovered a grand total of zero advertised yoga teaching jobs, but I knew better than to rely on ads. Almost every studio is constantly looking for teachers, even though they don't announce it. After two hours of research, I made a list of venues that looked interesting, and I started sending emails.

I received two noes and seven studios didn't respond at all, but then I received a bite from a studio that was under construction. Mark, one of the owners, emailed me back and we arranged a phone conversation to talk more in detail about his new venture. Mark and a couple friends had partnered to open a yoga studio right in Central, Hong Kong, the city's central business district. He freely admitted that he had no idea what he was doing when it came to yoga, but he knew they needed staff fast.

Mark was nervous about considering his first hire without meeting in person and doubly nervous because I was still such a new teacher. I couldn't possibly get to Hong Kong for a visit, so

I encouraged him to speak with my current employer. Later that week, my boss spoke with him at length and gave me a glowing recommendation. She didn't want me to quit obviously, but I'd earned her trust and she wanted to support my growth. I owe her a big debt of gratitude.

Ten days after our initial call, Mark sent me a preliminary work contract, and after dozens of administrative back-and-forth emails, I was legally employed in another country. I bought my plane tickets and moved to Hong Kong. From start to finish, the process took eight weeks.

You could say I'm just lucky, but remember, this was the second time I'd landed a job in a foreign country, sight unseen. Clearly, I was doing something right. My secret is that I understand the hiring process and present myself more professionally than my peers. In the yoga market, professionalism is so scarce that it'll give you a huge advantage.

Get Clear on Your Objective

Many yoga teachers take a "go with the flow" attitude to their working life. They relax into the rhythm of their schedule and allow the future to unfold as it will. If you choose this approach, I can tell you exactly what happens next—absolutely nothing. If you're a top teacher, your studio owner secretly hopes you'll continue doing exactly what you're doing now for as long as possible. If you're not a top teacher and you're struggling and waiting for the phone to ring, that too will most likely not change unless you take matters into your own hands.

As we've discussed in earlier chapters, there are currently more opportunities than ever, both inside and outside of traditional yoga settings, but those doors don't open themselves. To pry them open, you need to act like an independent professional and proactively pursue your goals.

It's often said that success is based on who you know, but if that were true, I'd be a total failure. Although I work with thousands of people each month, I have only a few real friends, and I mostly spend time with my immediate family. Despite my hermit-like lifestyle, I've landed amazing jobs, obtained free advice from *Fortune* 500 CEOs, and traveled and taught all around the world. I don't know how to network, but I do know how to knock politely on the right doors, and in the next section, I'll give you the tools to do the same.

FIND THE RIGHT PERSON

When conducting outreach, your job is to find the right person. Yoga teachers make the mistake of emailing info@website.com addresses or filling out "Contact Us" forms on websites. This amateur move makes it easy for prospective employers to ignore your message. Today, there is so much information available online that you can easily find the right person and message them directly.

I'm certain that if I'd emailed Mark's general studio address instead of emailing him personally, I would never have gotten the phone call or landed the job. The five extra minutes it took to track down Mark's personal email address made all the difference. Below is my best advice for quickly determining who is in charge of an organization and finding their contact details.

- **Yoga Studios.** Ninety percent of the time, the owner and manager are the same person. That individual is often listed first on the "About Us" page on the website. In many cases, the owner is the manager *and* the head teacher too. Their email address is almost always firstname@website.com.

- **Gyms.** Boutique and specialty gyms are exactly like yoga studios. Check the "About Us" page on the website, and you'll usually find the owner or manager easily. If you're looking at big-box gyms and franchise gyms, LinkedIn will provide better information. If all else fails, pick up the phone and ask who oversees hiring. Here's what to say: "Hi, I'm a yoga teacher and I'm wondering who is in charge of hiring trainers and instructors."

- **Nursing homes.** Many nursing homes will have a staff member with the job title Wellness Director. If you see one listed on their website or LinkedIn page, contact them. If you do not find anyone with that job title, contact anyone whose title on LinkedIn includes the word *director*, and don't be shy about contacting multiple people at the same facility.

- **Schools.** Public and private schools operate very differently, but the common job titles to look for include Athletic Director, Student Services Director, and Activities Director. In many schools, one of the teachers is unofficially in charge of extracurricular activities, so it can be challenging to know where to start. If you are unsure, pick up the phone and ask. Here's what to say: "Hi, I'm a yoga teacher, and I'm wondering who is in charge of after-school activities and events."

- **Corporate classes.** In smaller companies, your best option is to contact the owner directly. In larger companies, those with a human resources department, you'll want to target the Director of Human Resources. The actual decisions are usually made by individual department heads, but Human Resources often gets involved, so start there.

- **Hotels.** If you're targeting a boutique hotel, contact the general manager directly. If you're contacting a large hotel, the only person you should reach out to is the concierge. This person will rarely have a company email address, so you'll either need to call and ask to be transferred, or simply walk into the hotel and speak to them in person. Here's what to say: "Hi, I'm a yoga teacher. I'm calling to see if your clients ever ask for private yoga classes during their stays."

- **Health resorts.** Most health resorts are independently owned, so the decision maker is usually not too hard to find. The Spa Manager, Hotel Manager, or Guest Services Manager can all be potential contacts. If you're unsure, give them a call. Here's what to say: "I noticed you offer yoga classes at your resort. Can I ask who oversees hiring teachers?"

How to Send Cold Emails

Below, you'll find sample emails for classes, workshops, and other teaching gigs. You'll obviously want to edit the details to make them personal to you, but don't be tempted to edit too much. No purple font, no prayer-hand emojis, no inspirational quotes, and no photo attachments. Remember, you're knocking on doors. Be polite, be direct, and follow the process step by step.

TEMPLATE ONE: STUDIO TEACHING JOB PITCH

SUBJECT: *Are you looking for yoga teachers?*

Dear NAME,

Are you looking for yoga teachers at XYZ Studio?

I took a class last week at XYZ Studio with Amelia, and I loved it. I really appreciated how her sequence was accessible and still very challenging. As a Vinyasa Flow instructor, I teach very similar classes myself, and I'd love to be part of your team.

Thanks in advance for your consideration!

Sincerely,

Your Name

YogaBody.bio/yourname

TEMPLATE TWO: GYM WORKSHOP PITCH

SUBJECT: *Yoga for Deep Sleep at XYZ Fitness?*

Dear NAME,

Would you be interested in hosting a Yoga for Deep Sleep workshop at XYZ Fitness?

In my workshops, I guide students through breathing exercises and singing bowl sound meditation, and then we finish with a guided relaxation. The event is ninety minutes long, and as you can imagine, students LOVE this experience.

Would this potentially be interesting to you?

Thanks for your consideration.

Sincerely,

Your Name

YogaBody.bio/yourname

TEMPLATE THREE: NURSING HOME PITCH

SUBJECT: *Golden Years Yoga at XYZ Nursing Home?*

Dear NAME,

Would you be interested in offering your residents Golden Years Yoga classes?

My mother was moved to a nursing facility three years ago, and she missed coming to my weekly yoga classes. At her request, I began teaching chair-based yoga at her facility, and it lifted the spirits and energy of all the students. I've since formalized the program into a biweekly forty-five-minute class that incorporates gentle seated movements, guided breathwork, and mindfulness without religion.

Would this be something that might interest your residents?

Sincerely,

Your Name

YogaBody.bio/yourname

TEMPLATE FOUR: HIGH SCHOOL PITCH

SUBJECT: *Teen Yoga for Productivity and Focus at XYZ School?*

Dear NAME,

Would you be interested in offering Teen Yoga for Productivity and Focus at XYZ School?

With all the distractions coming from their phones and social media, kids struggle more than ever to focus on their schoolwork. I teach a moving mindfulness practice that incorporates breathing and yoga postures. It gives teenagers the self-care tools they need to regain control over their minds.

Would this be potentially interesting to you?

Sincerely,

Your Name

YogaBody.bio/yourname

**TEMPLATE FIVE: UNIVERSITY PROFESSIONAL
CERTIFICATION PITCH**

SUBJECT: *Yoga for Stress Certification Course at XYZ
University?*

Dear NAME,

*Would you be interested in offering a Yoga for Stress
Management certification course as an elective?*

*I know your undergraduates at XYZ University are offered
electives in workplace wellness, so I thought my Yoga Alliance-
registered training course might be a unique offering.*

*It's a three-day program that takes an evidence-based approach
to stress management.*

Would this be potentially interesting?

Sincerely,

Your Name

YogaBody.bio/yourname

TEMPLATE SIX: CORPORATE CLIENT PITCH

SUBJECT: *Office Yoga at XYZ Corp?*

Dear NAME,

Would you be interested in offering your team Office Yoga?

Before teaching, I spent eight years at an advertising agency, and my shoulders and hamstrings got so stiff that I felt like I was aging at double speed.

Yoga helped me undo the stress accumulated from years of desk work, and I now teach Office Yoga for both physical and mental stress release. No yoga clothes or yoga mats required. I lead teams through simple poses right at their workstations or in a conference room.

Would this potentially be of interest?

Sincerely,

Your Name

YogaBody.bio/yourname

TEMPLATE SEVEN: HOTEL CONCIERGE PITCH

SUBJECT: *Private Yoga Classes at XYZ Hotel?*

Dear NAME,

Do your guests ever ask about yoga classes?

I teach dynamic yoga, deep stretching, and mindfulness. For hotel guests, I bring all my own mats and props, so it couldn't be easier.

If you have a guest whom you think would be interested, please call or message me anytime: xxx-xxx-xxxx.

I will happily give you a 10 percent commission on all my bookings.

Sincerely,

Your Name

YogaBody.bio/yourname

TEMPLATE EIGHT: HEALTH RESORT PITCH

SUBJECT: *Looking for Yoga Teachers at XYZ Resort?*

Dear NAME,

Would you be interested in offering your guests Yoga for Mind-Body Balance?

Most people who choose health-centered holidays are overworked, overfed, and overwhelmed. To combat this, I teach science-based yoga and breathing classes designed to reduce cortisol levels, normalize breathing, and instill present-moment mindfulness.

Would classes like this benefit your guests?

Sincerely,

Your Name

YogaBody.bio/yourname

The Initial Call or Meeting

During cold email outreach sessions, a high response rate is around 10 percent. It's a mistake to interpret a lack of response or a no response as anything personal. In fact, many times those same people will reach out to you months later and suddenly show interest. When you receive positive replies, politely suggest a telephone call or in-person meeting as quickly as possible.

The most common mistake that people make in interviews—all interviews, not only yoga—is trying to impress their potential employer with how great they are. The way to impress your potential employer is to show them that you're paying attention to *their* needs. When they ask questions about you, give a direct and honest answer but very quickly, bounce back with a question of your own.

Questions to Ask:
- Who are your most popular teachers? And why?
- Who are your best clients? And why?
- What is your busiest class right now?
- What is the biggest challenge for you right now?
- How has your vision for the studio changed since when you started?

Chances are, no interviewee has ever asked these types of questions before. When you do, your potential employer will probably open up to you, giving you honest, valuable information about what works for them and what they find challenging. You can also use their answers to clearly articulate how your strengths meet their needs.

If you learn that their star teacher leads a dynamic vinyasa class, for example, you can talk about your athletic flow classes.

If their most popular session is meditation based, you can speak about your meditation teachings. Of course, only share things that are true. This is not an invitation to lie; instead, it's a smart way to ensure that the conversation is positive.

I've personally hired more than 150 yoga teachers in my career, and I've never hired someone because of their certificate or their advanced practice. Multiple times, I've hired freshly certified teachers instead of experienced colleagues simply because they were more professional.

Proper Etiquette: Email, Phone, and Attire

The yoga industry is very casual. We're often barefoot in yoga pants, so it's no surprise that many teachers default to casual email and phone conversations, and many neglect to think about their physical appearance. Just like in any job, however, these little things matter.

In emails, don't write in all lower case or use funny fonts or colors. No emojis or huge attachments. Make sure you're writing in complete sentences with a proper opening salutation and closing message. Even if the person you're communicating with sends you fragmented messages obviously written on their phone while on the go, hold the line and keep your communication formal and professional.

During phone conversations, make sure you're in a quiet place, not a busy gym or coffee shop. For in-person meetings, wear clean yoga clothes in good condition. Pull your hair out of your face, and make sure you look the part.

Navigating Trial Classes/Videos

It's common practice in the hiring process to be asked to conduct a trial class or to submit a sample teaching video. The idea is to allow your potential employer to see and hear you at work. Years ago, I interviewed a great applicant named Carlos for a teaching job. When we proceeded to his test class, everything went wrong. He spent half the session in the front of the room first demonstrating and then attempting to teach a handstand routine. He had a great practice, for sure, but the students didn't care. They were beginners, it was a Thursday morning, and the class was way over their heads.

Video submissions (in lieu of a test class) often exhibit the same problem. Teachers feel the need to impress by demonstrating their most extreme arm balances or flexibility poses. As a long-time student of yoga, these are always interesting to watch. As someone hiring teachers, they're not helpful. Employers are most interested in your voice, your body language, and your ability to lead a room of people.

The best trial classes or sample videos are extremely simple. Teach sun salutes, tree pose, and forward folds. Remember, almost every studio caters to beginners, so your trial class should focus on fundamentals.

Some other tips for trial classes or sample videos:
- Show up early/stay after class (if in person).
- Choose obvious, common poses.
- Don't test new material.
- Dress professionally.
- Pull your hair out of your face.
- Make sure your nails on your hands and feet are trimmed and clean.

- Brush your teeth before class.
- Demonstrate as little as possible.
- Use simple, clear language.
- Skip music completely (it's too much for a test class).
- Don't burn incense.
- No essential oils.

Scheduling

There's a big difference between professional scheduling conflicts and personal scheduling conflicts. Suppose you're offered a class at a new studio on Tuesday nights, but you have a long-standing private client at that same time. Alternatively, maybe the studio owner offers you a job starting next weekend, but you already have a local workshop planned at another venue. These schedule conflicts might be inconvenient, but they demonstrate that you are an in-demand working professional. It's okay.

Personal schedule conflicts, on the other hand, are often red flags. If you're offered a class on Tuesday nights, but you have a party this week that you don't want to miss, that's not something you should share. If you're offered a morning class, but you decline because you're not a morning person, it's unlikely there will be any other offers.

Remember, the yoga industry is filled with flaky personalities, so try to make yourself easy to work with and solution-oriented. It goes a long way.

Salaries and Contracts

For drop-in classes, most studios offer a fixed pay scale where top teachers might earn 20 percent or 25 percent more than newbies but rarely more. Most studios operate on a tight budget and don't have much room to negotiate. I've personally never met a studio owner or manager who purposefully tried to underpay their teachers. The sad truth is that studio owners often pay their teachers more than they pay themselves!

Despite the low pay for drop-in class work, many yoga teachers still accept these gigs because they are a great way to hone your craft, gain exposure to huge numbers of people, and have a lot of fun. Once your foot is in the door, you'll often discover other ways to generate more income, such as workshops, events, or teacher training programs.

If you're working for a yoga studio or gym, they'll often ask you to sign a work contract. Contracts are standard practice, and the only big thing to look out for is whether they try to include an exclusivity clause. If the studio is not able to offer you full-time pay, it's unethical (and, in many places, illegal) to request exclusivity, and yet many employers do ask. Don't agree to an exclusive arrangement.

Some studios will also limit or expect a percentage of side projects, outside of studio work, like private classes or retreats. Every situation is unique, but again, if your employer is not offering you a full-time opportunity, they should not ask you for this level of commitment.

In my experience, teachers who are open, honest, and transparent about their needs and concerns can usually find a win-win arrangement. In all cases, address any doubts or concerns before, not after, signing an agreement and starting work.

The Power of Professionalism

I had a graduate named Philip who took an extended leave from his administrative job working for the city of Toronto to become a yoga teacher. About halfway through his training, it was clear to him that he just could not return to his old work life—he was bored and burned out. At the same time, he didn't want to lose the amazing benefits and retirement plan offered to city employees.

His solution? What if he could figure out a way to teach yoga for the city? Philip spent a weekend cleaning up his résumé to reflect his yoga ambitions, and he wrote a very simple email to his former boss. Remember, at this point, Philip wasn't even a certified teacher!

As you can imagine, everything in the public sector is slow and complicated, but just two months after graduating as a certified teacher, Philip was given the title Wellness Consultant and essentially became the resident yoga teacher in half a dozen city offices. His hours were cut in half and his pay reduced, yes, but he was doing what he loved, he had plenty of time to pursue other work, and he was able to keep the benefits and connections from his previous career.

I'm sharing this story with you because Philip got the job not because he was the most qualified available teacher—he was barely even certified! He landed the job because of his connections and his professionalism. There are one hundred teachers in Toronto who would have lined up for that opportunity, yet it was Philip who secured it. It takes years to become a senior instructor, but it can take as little as a weekend of work to position yourself as the most professional person for a role. You can do the same as Philip and get the gig you want.

CHAPTER XII

How to Launch Your Business

A colleague named Vince developed a three-day training program and wanted my help with promotions. Vince knew I'd organized an open house for the studio where we both worked and thought something similar might be useful for his course. The open house was a casual Sunday afternoon gathering that included a yoga demonstration, refreshments, and music.

It was true that students had loved the open house, but I didn't see how this type of event could be used to promote a course. Although I didn't see the point, I agreed to help Vince anyway. We picked a date and started planning.

We used Microsoft Word to create a one-sided black-and-white flyer. The flyer featured a photo of Vince in butterfly pose, with the event details typed out below his feet. We posted the announcement on a bulletin board in the studio and at health food stores around town. Both Vince and I emailed a PDF version of the flyer to our respective contact lists. The entire process could not have been simpler.

Below is what the announcement looked like:

YOU'RE INVITED: *Yin Yoga Open House*

WHAT: *Yoga Demo, Q&A, Info Session, Chips & Guacamole*

WHEN: *Saturday, December 12, 2:00 p.m. to 3:30 p.m.*

COST: *Free! (+ bring a friend)*

RSVP: *email@domain.com*

On the day of the event, I was surprised to see eighteen people show up. They went straight for the food, as expected, but when Vince started his demo, they circled up and showed a clear interest in the yoga, not just the snacks.

Vince was much better at business than me, and he asked everyone to write their names on strips of paper. We tossed all the crinkled-up papers into a bowl and drew names, creating a makeshift lucky draw. Vince had come prepared: he gave away some silly prizes, like T-shirts and yoga books, but most of the prizes were freebies or discounts for his upcoming course. Finally, I understood. This event was genius.

Four people signed up and paid for the course that very day. A week later, six people who missed the party called for more information and signed up too. Finally, through word of mouth, an additional four students registered, paying full price. Vince was disappointed we didn't meet his goal of twenty sign-ups, but I was thrilled we had fourteen bookings. Amazing!

Throughout this book, you've worked on mindset, positioning, defining success, and setting goals, among other things. Now it's time to launch that vision into the world, just like Vince did. Perhaps you want to start teaching private clients from your living room, or maybe you're ready to expand your offerings to include workshops, retreats, corporate gigs, and training events.

Wherever you find yourself today, your biggest enemy is inertia. In every industry, the status quo has a strong pull, but it's particularly strong in yoga because there is no one to prod you forward, no corporate ladder to climb, and no one to answer to except yourself. In this chapter, I'll encourage you to push through that inertia and turn your ideas into reality using event-based marketing. We'll cover two distinct yet equally valuable approaches you can use to start a new venture on the right foot: the launch party strategy and the case study strategy.

188 • Yoga Business Mastery

The Launch Party Strategy

That open house marked a turning point for me because I realized that if I could help build a buzz for Vince's training, I could do the same for my own events too. A few months later, I did just that, and since then, I have hosted at least a dozen similar events, which I now refer to as launch parties. People have housewarming parties, bridal showers, and baby showers, so why not celebrate the birth of your new business venture too?

Here's how the launch party strategy works. First, pick a non-peak-social day of the week. Fridays and Saturdays are off-limits, since people will prioritize other events. Thursday evenings or Sunday afternoons work best. Next, make sure your launch party is short and sweet. Ninety minutes is the ideal length of time: enough for people to meet and mingle but not so much that they sacrifice a huge chunk of their day. Food is crucial. You can cook it yourself, buy it, or convince a local restaurant to donate, but whatever you do, make sure there are snacks. It's a good idea to play some music to create a vibe. Last, don't forget the lucky draw.

SAMPLE NINETY-MINUTE LAUNCH PARTY SCHEDULE

Here's a typical schedule for a launch party. I advise you to stick closely to this format. It works.

First thirty minutes: Arrival, snacks, lucky draw sign-up
Thirty to forty-five minutes: Yoga demo, Q&A sessions
Forty-five minutes until end: Lucky draw and info about your new projects

The best place to promote your launch party is through your existing community. Leverage your contacts on social media, email, and SMS. If you teach public classes, announce your launch party at the end of each session you teach during the ten days leading up to the event. Encourage anyone who is interested to bring a friend. If there are public bulletin boards around your town, post a simple flyer. If you're connected to any online or off-line social groups, invite those contacts too.

WHERE TO HOST THE PARTY?

Remember that ninety minutes flies by. Many people will arrive late, so the party will be over before you know it. For this reason, I encourage you to plan and prepare carefully, choosing the right venue and managing the itinerary skillfully.

I have hosted launch parties in the park, at my home, in yoga studios, and even in rented venues. I prefer indoor venues if possible because there are bathrooms, there's electricity for music, and it's easier to capture attention when the time comes for your demo, lucky draw, and announcements.

As people arrive, stand by the door and greet everyone. If you don't know their names, learn them, and allow for natural, social conversations. Have everyone write down their names for the lucky draw, and then send them to the food table so you can continue to greet newcomers. This is community building, not network marketing. Don't try to sell or pitch anyone; just be yourself and connect.

THE YOGA DEMO AND TALK

Yoga teachers hate demonstrations, but students love them, •
so do it. What should you demonstrate? Anything relevant.
If you're launching a stress management program, you might
share three mindfulness practices. If you're launching a yoga
for strength program, show guests some of the arm balances
you've mastered and a few tips as a preview of your workshop.
Your demonstration can be interactive, and if you focus on
teaching, not on entertaining, both you and your students will
feel more comfortable.

LUCKY DRAW DETAILS

You'll be tempted to skip the lucky draw—don't! People love it,
and it will determine the success of this event. Ideal giveaways
are of high value to students with little or no hard cost to you. As
top prizes, for example, you might offer a private yoga class or a
free slot at an upcoming workshop. Having one or two high-value
giveaways is a sign of goodwill and is in line with the true spirit
of a lucky draw. After that, you can offer discount coupons, which
will also be well received.

Discount prizes might include two-for-one offers or 30
percent, 20 percent, or 10 percent off yoga packages, events, or
whatever other offerings you might have available. Make it clear
that these prizes must have a twenty-four-hour validity window,
meaning people need to purchase now (or the next day) to secure
the discount. Without time pressure, no one will decide—and
worse, you might end up hearing from students who want to
redeem unused offers months or years down the line.

To create the prizes themselves, type out a personal letter to go with each offer, sign it, and place it in an envelope. Write the prize name on the outside of the envelope so you know what's inside, make a pile of envelopes, and you're ready to go. Be sure to prepare everything the day before the party so the lucky draw flows smoothly.

If you'd like to expand your lucky draw prizes beyond your own services, you can easily solicit prize donations from massage therapists, chiropractors, and even local restaurants in the area. I've done this many times and am always surprised by how generous most people are when asked. Just like you, these local businesses are looking for ways to promote themselves, and many will be excited to be part of the event.

Here's how a sample selection of prizes (twenty in total) might break down:

- 3 x Private Yoga Session
- 4 x 30 percent off Workshop Series
- 6 x 20 percent off Private Yoga (4, 8, or 12 sessions)
- 5 x 10 percent off Monthly Membership
- 1 x T-shirt
- 1 x Yoga Mat

One final tip: keep the lucky draw moving. If you go slowly and watch everyone open their envelopes like Christmas presents, the situation will feel awkward. Instead, grab someone to assist you in passing out the prizes. In a rapid-fire pattern, draw names and call out the winners. This flurry of giveaways is fast and fun. From start to finish, you should distribute all your prizes in just a few minutes.

ANNOUNCE YOUR LAUNCH

Straight after your lucky draw, while you still have everyone's attention, thank them for coming and share an update on your new venture. People love announcements of new things, so if you're launching a private yoga business or workshop series, explain why you're excited about it and how it represents an exciting transition for you as a teacher. Better still, share with them the benefits they might obtain by signing up. Remember, this is your launch party, so take the time to tell everyone what you're doing. Here's what a sample announcement might look like:

> *Thanks, everyone, for coming today! I really appreciate all your support. If you're not yet following me on social media, please find me @YourName. Just to let you know, I have a mindfulness workshop next weekend. A couple of you got free tickets in the lucky draw, so I hope you can make it. My weekly classes at XYZ Studio will continue next month, and most importantly, I'm accepting bookings for my New You in the New Year Retreat. Today's party is officially over, but feel free to hang out, ask questions, and enjoy. Thanks again for coming, and I hope to see you in class soon!*

From Zero to Local Hero

I had a graduate named Lorraine who transformed a shed in her backyard into a cute little hot yoga studio with space for six mats. Her suburban neighborhood was home to nearly fourteen hundred residents, but the nearest gym was miles away, so Lorraine knew that if she could only spread the word, there would be a high demand for her classes and an opportunity to increase her income.

What did she do? She threw a simple launch party.

Although Lorraine was new to the area, she was friendly with her neighbors on either side. She also knew three moms from her daughter's school. She gave everyone a handwritten invite. A local recreation center had a bulletin board, so Lorraine posted a flyer there. Last, she went online, found two local groups on social media, and received permission from the admins to share her event.

The party was scheduled for a Sunday afternoon, and Lorraine was delighted when nine people showed up. Per my suggestion, she had everyone write down their names for a lucky draw. She served tea and cookies in the garden, and after people had introduced themselves, she gave them a tour of her little studio and demonstrated three poses specifically for the knees—her particular area of interest.

The lucky draw was smooth but uneventful. She gifted a private class to one woman, a two-class pack to another, and discount cards to the remaining guests. That day, no one bought anything, and Lorraine emailed me feeling defeated. She was worried she'd wasted her time.

I asked whether she'd included a twenty-four-hour validity on the discount cards, and Lorraine confirmed that she had. The very next day, one of the moms who had received a 20-percent-off voucher at the party called to book classes for the following week and asked sheepishly whether she could use the same discount offer for three of her friends, who were also interested. Lorraine bit her lip and said, "Yes, of course!"

Lorraine's little studio offered a total of just four classes per week, Monday through Thursday; that first week, she taught the same four moms every single afternoon. By the second week, word had spread, and her remaining two mats were occupied. Within a month, Lorraine had a three-month waiting list just to take a class.

Although that sounds impossibly lucky, remember, Lorraine's capacity was just six mats, four days a week, and most of her students booked for every single class. Even though her capacity was small, Lorraine's per-class revenue was more than triple what she had earned previously at a studio across town. No more commuting to work, no more fighting for her ideal schedule. Lorraine went from zero to local hero in a matter of weeks.

The Case Study Strategy

Often, I work with yoga teachers who have the seed of an idea for a new workshop series or intensive course, but they are not 100 percent ready to launch. Maybe they need more research, maybe they need more practice, or maybe they simply lack confidence. I've been in this position myself half a dozen times, and I solved the problem using another great event-based marketing strategy called a yoga case study.

The purpose of hosting a yoga case study is threefold: (1) to get your idea out of your head and into the world fast, (2) to gather real feedback and testimonials from clients, and (3) to earn some money as you go. You can offer the case study free of charge, but I find that if people don't pay, many will drop out. My preferred method is to tell people directly that the study is a new workshop I'm launching that will cost $X, but as a case study participant, they can join for 50 percent off. As another benefit, they'll be part of a private group of just eight students in total.

Why call it a case study? Because that's what it is. You're learning, they're learning, it's a work in progress. Plus, people love case studies. They love to be part of something new because it's exciting. Just think: people line up for the premiere of a movie the day it opens. The next day, the theater will be empty. Why? It's fun! People will put a deposit down for a car that is not going to be released for months or even a year or more. Why? New things are exciting! Tap into that excitement, take some pressure off yourself, and use this simple formula to soft launch a new program.

Promote your case study just as you did your launch party. Use social media, bulletin boards, emails, and your phone to let people know. Often, I tell participants that I'll be asking for their honest feedback at the end of the case study, but I let them know it'll be totally optional. This way, if things go well, students are not at all surprised when I ask for a written testimonial or video message about their experiences—and many provide one without even being asked.

I encourage you to restrict the case study to a total of four sessions—no more. It can also be helpful to limit the number of participants so you don't feel overwhelmed. I'd also encourage you to deliver the entire workshop over a maximum time frame of two weeks to create an intensive feel. This is enough time to go deeply into your subject but not such a big commitment that people will need to turn their lives upside down to participate.

Tuesday and Thursday evenings can be convenient times for classes, and I have had success with weekend sessions as well. Since these are your charter customers, you should pull out all the stops and overdeliver. Use this opportunity to do your best work. Make yourself fully available, even between scheduled sessions, and give your case study your absolute best effort.

In business, we all tend to overthink and overcomplicate things. Both the launch party and case study force you to keep things simple, focus on grassroots marketing, and get your teaching in front of an audience fast. If you're nervous to launch, it's normal, and there are two reasons for this. The first reason people are nervous is because they're unprepared. If that's the case, get to work and prepare yourself. The second and more common reason teachers are nervous is because they care. You want to be useful, provide value, and ultimately deliver a great class experience. If this is why you're nervous, that's good. Be nervous, pick a date on the calendar, and get going!

Example Case Studies

Let's imagine you want to specialize in yoga for healthy shoulders because you yourself have had a rotator cuff injury. Perhaps, through your own healing process, you learned some very powerful techniques you'd like to share. Although you anticipate that a four-part workshop will be the ideal format, you're still fleshing out the details. Here's how you might launch that as a case study.

Case Study Participants Wanted: *Yoga for Healthy Shoulders*

Are you suffering from a rotator cuff injury that just doesn't seem to heal? If so, I'm recruiting case study participants to join my four-part Yoga for Healthy Shoulders program, where I'll share with you the stretches, strengthening exercises, and anti-inflammatory foods that made all the difference when I healed my own shoulder.

Interested? Please email me personally, email@domain.com, for details.

Here are some other ideas of case studies you might consider:

- Yoga for Weight Loss Case Study
- Yoga for Back Pain Case Study
- Yoga for Deep Sleep Case Study
- Yoga for Stress Management Case Study
- Yoga for Attention and Focus Case Study

The Yoga for Back Pain Case Study

Teresa lived in a small town of just seventy-five hundred people. She was a newly certified Yoga Trapeze instructor, bursting with energy to teach, and yet, she knew her small town offered only a very limited audience. To make matters more challenging, there was an inexpensive municipal gym in the area that offered yoga classes and had a pool, among other facilities. Teresa considered partnering with the gym to offer her classes, but the salaries they offered to instructors were ridiculously low.

What did she do instead? A case study on yoga for back pain.

Teresa was a longtime fitness fanatic, but in her early forties, chronic lower back problems forced her to change her routine. She stopped lifting heavy and logging so many road-running miles. Instead, she explored dance fitness, bodyweight training, and suspension yoga on the Yoga Trapeze. As it turned out, she was in love with her new routine and most delighted about how suspension yoga helped heal her spine. Her main motivation for teaching Yoga Trapeze was back care, making it a logical theme for her case study.

Here's what she did. In her living room, Teresa installed five rigs. It was tight but cozy, and since there were windows on two sides, it didn't feel claustrophobic. Next, she and a friend spent an afternoon snapping photos of Teresa in her favorite spinal decompression poses. They also took pictures of the practice space itself, pictures of Teresa with her teaching certificate, and some shots of her home from the street to help tell the visual story of this new venture.

Teresa pitched her story to her local paper. They didn't run it in their print edition, but they did post a very thorough write-up in their online edition and shared it on social media. The newspaper was kind enough to provide links to Teresa's social media accounts. When she saw new followers and engagement activity online, Teresa immediately started promoting her Yoga for Back Care Case Study. On her social accounts, she solicited students for a two-week intensive for anyone with chronic lower back pain. She offered the case study series for ninety-nine dollars, and all five spots sold in just three days.

Teresa was excited by the quick success but nervous to launch this program, especially considering that it would be a semiprivate class with just five students. She prepared and practiced diligently. If anything, she overprepared, but it was time well spent because she was organized and confident for each session.

One student dropped out after the first week due to a family health problem, but the remaining four not only finished the program; they also wrote glowing reviews that Teresa used to sell her next intake—not as a case study but as a two-week intensive priced at $199.

Conclusion

Over lunch one day, a yoga teacher friend, Kevin, was lamenting the fact that his brother earned more than him working as a waiter. Kevin was teaching seven to ten classes a week but still couldn't afford to live on his own—he had roommates.

Kevin finished his rant by saying, "One thing I love about being a yoga teacher is that at least you know you'll never make any money, so you can let go of that ambition and accept your life as it is."

It was a beautiful sentiment: give up the striving, take what comes, focus on teaching, and go with the flow. But Kevin is still in the first half of his life, single, and hasn't yet been confronted with the inevitable stacking of responsibilities (and rewards) that come with age. The moment you have a sick relative, a new baby, or a team of employees to pay, this idealized view of money and business suddenly goes out the window. Money matters, business can expand your influence and impact, and deep down, growth is hardwired into the human experience.

Many people in the yoga community will echo clichés such as "Go with the flow," "If you do what you love, the money will follow," or "Everything works out in the end." The reality is much more prosaic and less poetic. If you're working an entry-level job teaching Tuesday and Thursday classes at a local studio, you will receive entry-level pay. When you branch out to specialized work and explore nontraditional teaching settings, you will immediately be able to double, triple, or even quintuple your rates. As you grow into expert-level teaching that includes workshops, events, and training courses, your financial earnings and influence will again multiply. This type of career progression does not happen by going with the flow; instead, it's the result of planning, learning, and conscious creation.

My friend Kevin had accepted his plight as a broke yoga teacher. Unfortunately, the world doesn't want or need any more broke yoga teachers. All those roles have been filled for decades. Today, the world needs creative, career-focused, service-oriented teachers who are excited to grow professionally and teach their growing communities. My challenge to you is to step into that higher echelon of value, both for yourself and for your students.

You picked up this book because you knew that success as a yoga teacher was possible, but you wanted a plan to help turn that abstract truth into a realized truth. In Chapter I, you learned the importance of emptying your head trash, deconstructing negative beliefs, and finding new inspirations for a growth-oriented future. In Chapter II, we reviewed the essential skills for yoga teachers. The best teachers are lifelong learners, and your path to professional growth should be focused on the needs of your students and your personal passions, not arbitrary credentials.

Next, we explored the importance of developing a unique teaching positioning. This is a chapter worth grappling with and always keeping top of mind. When you plant your flag in the ground and establish a unique positioning in the market, this is when you'll unlock your best life. Chapter IV focused on the only two assets that have any true value in the yoga business: you and your community. You should focus most of your time on developing your skills, knowledge, and abilities, along with building relationships with the people who know, like, and trust you. Avoid distractions like logos, personal branding, and taglines. Focus on the highest-leverage areas of value in this business and you'll find success quickly.

In Chapter V, you defined teaching success on your terms. What does your ideal teaching life look like? How much would you like to earn? How much do you *need* to earn? Focus on the five Ws: why, what, who, where, when. Define these objectives and you'll establish a North Star to keep you moving in a direction that fulfills your goals.

Chapter VI focused on *where* to teach: studios, gyms, fitness centers, and schools. Yoga has gone mainstream, and you learned that there are now more teaching jobs outside of studios than inside and more opportunities than you realized. There are infinite options to collaborate with companies and dozens of opportunities to work for yourself too.

In Chapter VII, you learned how to use your phone and a laptop to teach online from anywhere. In terms of lifestyle freedom, online teaching can be a game changer. Many teachers feel that they must choose between in-person and online teaching, but why force yourself to choose? You can do both!

Nothing we've discussed thus far is possible without an investment of time, so in Chapter VIII, we developed a very simple strategy to "feed the dragon" by investing one hour daily into the *you* asset and one hour daily into the *your community* asset of your business. When left unfed, your business starves; when consistently fed, it grows predictably and consistently every week.

For many yoga teachers, pricing and packaging services feels opaque and complex, but neglecting this element of business guarantees financial uncertainty. In Chapter IX, you learned about the importance of low-friction introductory offers and tiered pricing. You learned how to follow simple strategic principles to create win-win-win scenarios where your clients are happy, you feel your work is valued, and you receive appropriate remuneration.

You know that your students and potential employers will Google search your name, so your online profile is an important part of your professional image. In Chapter X, you learned simple strategies to help your profiles appear in search results, to clean up your image, and to present yourself in the best possible light.

In Chapter XI, you learned proven outreach strategies for landing teaching gigs, and you also received copy-and-paste templates you can quickly use for your business. Remember to keep it simple, find the decision maker, and aim to be of service. Although it's true that there are hundreds of thousands of yoga teachers, very few are actively seeking out opportunities and pitching prospective partners and employers. When you do this, you'll immediately be rewarded with opportunities others never even knew existed.

Now it's time to launch. You've done the heavy lifting and prep work. You have new ideas for classes, workshops, or private package offerings. You're now ready to welcome your first paying clients. In Chapter XII, you learned two proven go-to market strategies that cost little or no money but capture attention and revenue quickly. The case study is a powerful soft launch plan for new programs, and the launch party is a fun and effective strategy you can use again and again.

In all likelihood, you skimmed some chapters and lingered on others. If you're like most readers, you went deeper on the chapters you felt were most relevant to you right now. That's a smart choice. Success loves speed, and to that end, move fast, take action, and know you can always refer back to this book or the accompanying online resources to further grow and develop as a yoga business professional.

If you've gotten this far but remain stuck with analysis paralysis, here is my suggestion. Go back and choose one assignment or strategy that feels easy and achievable. Do that right now. Next, choose one task that feels difficult or that sparks a high level of internal resistance. Dig into that one next. Toggle back and forth between easy and challenging assignments, and most importantly, keep moving.

I had a student named Phoebe who told me that she was anti-business. As a teenager, she was a punk rock anarchist, and although she'd grown out of that phase, she still struggled to charge appropriately for her services. Phoebe initially fell in love with yoga as a way to manage her lifelong scoliosis, so uncovering her unique teaching positioning was easy: yoga for scoliosis. What she found hard was pricing.

I suggested she simply copy and paste one of the pricing grids in the online resource area: YogaBody.com/yogabusiness. Reluctantly, she did so. She stopped selling single classes and switched to four-session minimums. Instead of paying after each session, her clients now paid at the beginning of the month. The clients didn't mind the change; some even liked it better. And for Phoebe, the shift was enormous. She now knew exactly what she would earn early each month, and she could finally relax and enjoy her teaching without obsessing over bills.

Another reader, Gabrielle, had been teaching local outdoor groups successfully and got in touch in anticipation of the end of the summer season. Colder weather meant she needed to shift her focus for the off-season. She started with Chapter IV: Where to Teach and quickly decided to renovate and convert her garage into a semiprivate studio. That was her easy choice. Additionally, I challenged her to explore online teaching, something she found very difficult. She didn't like technology. Right away, the garage studio was a success, and much to her surprise, Gabrielle soon started a Sunday livestream class in that same space, which quickly reached more than three hundred concurrent viewers.

Last, I'll share with you Gerard's story. He got in touch before this book was finished. I sent him Chapter III: Positioning for Success and Chapter XI: Get the Gig. Gerard wanted to move away from studio vinyasa classes and instead target corporate clients, with a focus on breathing and mindfulness. On a Thursday night, he sent thirty pitch emails to various CEOs and heads of human resources departments in his area. By Monday, he had received four responses, and within a week he had booked his first gig. He attracted 263 people to his first breathing and mindfulness session, and his per-session rate was higher than his previous weekly earnings. Success!

Now it's your turn. Start right now, utilizing all the training and resources you have. Leverage the contacts and community you have today, and put one foot in front of the other, building, earning, and growing as you step further down the path.

Remember to visit www.YogaBody.com/yogabusiness to access the most current online resources. If you need help, please message me (@lucasrockwood) on social media, and send me your success stories too. I'd love to hear from you.

The business life of a yoga teacher can feel lonely at times, but please know that you're among a small but empowered group of instructors around the world actively working to build high-impact, high-earning businesses. You're not alone. I believe in you, and I'm cheering for you. Now go build your business.

Glossary

Below is a quick reference guide of terms and phrases referenced in the book as well as terms not mentioned but potentially relevant to your business life.

Unique Teaching Positioning (UTP). Think of this as your special sauce as a yoga teacher. What makes you unique, differentiated, and helps you add value rather than compete with the market?

You Asset. In the yoga business, the you asset refers to your skills, experiences, knowledge, and abilities.

Your Community. These are the people who know, like, and trust you. They might be phone contacts, social media followers, or subscribers to your email list.

Biznaz. Personal branding, taglines, logos, and color schemes, which are of secondary importance and do not constitute real business assets, hence the moniker, Biznaz.

Yoga Alliance. Not one but a group of unconnected, nonprofit trade registries that help organize yoga teachers and yoga schools.

Although not a formal registry, union, or trade organization, they do offer some oversight and resources for the industry.

Energetic Equity. Trust, engagement, and interest that accrues over time among students in your classes, on your email list, or on social media. Just like home equity, energetic equity has a real-world cash value that can often be realized easily through higher-value and higher-engagement class experience.

Entry-Level Job. In the yoga business, group classes at a studio are an entry-level job and will provide entry-level pay with a very real ceiling for earnings.

The 5 Ws. When planning for your career in life, it's helpful to define specifically the details of your ambition in terms of why, who, what, where, and when.

Buy Back Your Time. As you increase your income, you can use a portion of that earnings to free up more time to become more productive by hiring part-time help to assist you with time-consuming tasks like housework, laundry, and food prep.

Introductory Offer. In yoga, we aim to have an introductory offer that is so appealing that new students make a commitment to more than one class on their first day.

Cold Outreach. When you contact someone you don't know via phone, email, or in person, that is a cold outreach.

Launch Party. Just as a baby shower celebrates a forthcoming child, a launch party celebrates the birth of a new business.

Lucky Draw. Similar to a lottery, this is an event where you give away prizes based on names drawn at random from entries.

Case Study. A yoga case study is a way to soft launch a new class, workshop, or training event to a select group of people.

Return on Investment (ROI). If you invest $100 in one thousand printed flyers for an event and your flyers generate a total of $300, your ROI is 300 percent, or three times your initial outlay.

70/30 Split. The standard split for yoga teachers and venues for special events, workshops, and training events is 70 percent to the teacher and 30 percent to the venue after expenses. Exceptions always apply, of course.

Flatline Pricing. Consumers loathe bait-and-switch pricing where they are offered a great deal at first but then their rates go up massively later. Flatline pricing is a strategy where you attempt to make a great offer initially and then continue to meet or beat the offer in the future but simply ask for a greater purchase commitment.

Cost of Doing Business. Although everyone should aim to keep their costs as low as possible, there are certain costs of doing business that are unavoidable: taxes, merchant processing fees, rent, etc.

Top Line or Gross Revenue. This refers to the total money collected without deducting any expenses.

Bottom Line or Net Profit. This refers to all the money left over after you've paid all your bills.

Profit Margin. This refers to the money left over after expenses. If you generated $250 for a Saturday workshop and paid $50 to rent the pace, your margin would be $200.

Liability Waiver/New Student Form. This is the mandatory paperwork you should require for all students who join your class. It should solicit contact details, liability waiver, and an agreement of your terms of service. For free templates, visit www.yogabody. com/business.

Liability Insurance. Most yoga teachers should have personal liability insurance, regardless of whether the venue where they are teaching has coverage as well. Insurance for yoga teachers is extremely inexpensive, and a list of options can be found at www. yogabody.com/insurance.

Made in the USA
Monee, IL
20 December 2022

23196812R00135